Fonograf Editions

Fonograf Editions
Portland, OR

Cover and text design by Mike Corrao

First Edition, First Printing

FONO15

Published by Fonograf Editions
www.fonografeditions.com

For information about permission to reuse any material from this book, please contact Fonograf Ed. at info@fonografeditions.com.

ISBN: 978-1-7378036-5-2

FE

FONO
GRAF
FONOGRAF EDITIONS

Foreword

Originally published in 1927, Russian painter Kasimir Malevich's book *The Non-Objective World* delineates his vision that the best art values, above everything else, the "supremacy of pure feeling." According to Malevich there are "[t]wo basic types of creation [that] can be distinguished: one, initiated by the conscious mind, serves practical life, so-called, and deals with concrete visual phenomena; the other, stemming from the subconscious or superconscious mind, stands apart from all "practical utility" and treats abstract visual phenomena."

The cover design for this magazine is indebted to Malevich's Suprematist artistic vision, one that believed that "the appropriate means of representation is always the one which gives fullest possible expression to feeling as such and which ignores the familiar appearance of objects."

As editors, in putting this issue together, Malevich's maxims became our own. We sought work that seemed to challenge us in multiple ways, ways that we couldn't have predicted prior to reading. Included herein are novel excerpts and essays, poems, runes and translations. Our hope in including such a wide variety of work is that it speaks to Fonograf's own multifarious nature. What we like is entirely tempered by what we can hear and see and feel.

Thank you for reading.

— Jeff Alessandrelli, Adie Bovee, John Goodhue, Editors

TABLE OF CONTENTS

Andre Perry

The Blues

I had been kissing Jen up against a wall underneath a staircase in a dour cement building at the American School of Paris for two weeks. The first time it happened, we had packed up slowly after French class on the second floor. She put her books in her bag and then left the classroom. I waited for the rest of the students to leave, then the teacher. When it felt safe, I walked down the stairs and instead of running outside like everyone else I curved around the stairs and walked under the overhang. There she was, in her black puffy jacket and white jeans. We looked at each other briefly. She smiled. We didn't say a word. I walked up to her, our faces close, her short breaths blowing against my nose. I sunk my mouth into hers and it opened up like a flower to the sun. Her arms wrapped around my gawky, thin frame. After a minute I opened my eyes to see if her eyes were open too. They were closed and I spied on her face for a few moments before closing my eyes again. I eased my hands over her chest on the outside of her shirt. She sighed and a synapse, it seemed, exploded at the back of my head. We pulled away from each other. Jen smiled again and wiped her hand across her face where our saliva had collected. She picked up her book-bag and walked out from our hiding place. She adjusted her face, looking confident and spunky as she always did, and walked out of the building. My crotch was simmering. I took my bag and headed to the bus pick-up. I got on my bus, headed back to the 15th, and sat in the back with my friends. I didn't say a word about my adventure. Kristofor from Croatia turned on his boombox and we listened to the Clash because he said they were the best band in the world.

I was at lunch with Pat, Georgia and the rest of the boys. It was a few days after my first encounter with Jen. A Spartan atmosphere permeated the cafeteria as if it had been built to contain cadets or juvenile delinquents. I typically ate French fries, some baguette and butter and maybe the chicken or fish if it didn't look too dangerous. The fries and the baguette were reliable. One of our classmates walked by and Pat hunched over our table and quietly said, "I wonder what she tastes like." We all giggled. At a base level, we knew this kind of talk was wrong. We were also enthralled.

"I bet she's like apple pie," he continued quietly. "Made with bitter, bitter apples."

Our table roared with laughter. Pat picked away at his dead fish and then lifted his head one more time to address us, "But I would still have her anyway. Two helpings." The laughter continued. Georgia peeked up at us from his round spectacles.

"You guys are sick," he said.

"Fuck you, man," Pat said. Georgia just laughed it off. His name was David but we called him Georgia because the unmistakable drawl of his home-state amazed us every time he opened his mouth. A lot of us were American, the kids of expatriate parents—middle-class US diplomats, rich international businessmen, and post-hippie idealists who sought dreams beyond American shores. Maybe a third of the kids' parents worked for Disney and its Euro Disney project, a big mouse-eared amusement park they were building outside of town.

"How's that Zeppelin tape?" Georgia asked me.

"Shit, I'm sorry. One of these days." I had stolen his *Led Zeppelin I* cassette tape. I also had his copy of *Presence*. He had made a mistake in lending me those tapes. I had given his other stuff back, R.E.M. and They Might Be Giants, but the Zeppelin tapes, as far as I could see, were going to be mine for a long time.

"Don't worry about it," Georgia said. He was tiny, looked like he was in the fifth grade. I knew I would have to dig up something from my collection to lend him. Our friends all traded tiny remnants of pop culture-music, comics, and pornography if we could find it. Sometimes we got it back and sometimes these items were simply passed along to new owners. We were like community libraries for each other. Pat was always taking my comic books.

"Thanks Georgia, it's the best tape I've got right now," I said.

Jen and her friend Megan walked up to our table, carrying trays of French fries. "What are you little fucks up to?" she asked.

My pulse surged. Her presence gripped me. It felt as if my heart was going to erupt and spew out of my mouth. "Do you think we could sit down with y'all?" A couple of boys pushed over and she and Megan sat at the edge of our table. They didn't pay any special attention to me, just said hi to all of us at once. My young mind had worked relentlessly to define what made people attractive. Jen had arrived fully-formed—a magnet pulling on my budding hormones. Her dark blond hair blew out backwards, long and frizzy like the Bride of Frankenstein. Her face was a collection of miniature beauties: striking, small eyes like a pair of rich, dark marbles, a cute button of a nose protruding from her lightly-tanned face, a minor patch of freckles scattered across her cheeks, and a petite mouth with tender, reserved lips. But it was her spirit that grasped my attention, kept me rapt. In that remarkable distance between sixth and seventh grade Jen had achieved some transformation in attitude that made her seem older than everyone in the room. She tossed her plate of fries to the edge of her tray.

"This food tastes like shit," she said.

Pat laughed and said, "You're not trying hard enough."

"Oh, Pat, you're so cute. You can have my fries if you want them."

I knew she was only being sarcastic but something wild came over me. I wanted to hit Pat in the jaw when she called him *cute*. I locked eyes with Megan. She was eating her fries, looking at me to see if I was looking at Jen. Megan smiled.

Pat reached over another boy and grabbed Jen's tray. "Fuck yeah, I'll eat 'em."

Jen shrieked, "No Pat, I was joking." She reached up to grab her tray back and Pat, seeing the opportunity for spectacle, kept tugging at the tray, pulling it in his direction but not so hard as to overpower her. They tugged back and forth, the tray of fries hovering above the heads of the boys below. The game only lasted a few moments but each motion, the tray moving back in forth in either direction, was clear and concise. Jen let out one huge tug and Pat relinquished. The tray shifted toward Jen, the fries and the plate springing into the air and then onto the floor and table. The plate didn't break but it produced a wild clang as it hit the floor. The cafeteria staff looked up and mumbled French hatred beneath their breaths–to be the servants of these petulant American children was a curse.

"Well fuck, Pat, what am I going to do now?" Jen mugged at Pat trying to look angry. Pat shrugged his shoulders putting on his innocent face.

Georgia blurted out, "You guys are assho's," his Southern accent so thick that it elicited a laugh from the rest of the table.

Jen stood up and grabbed her book-bag. "I've got class and I'm not cleaning that up." Pat and a couple of other boys stood up too and grabbed their bags, ignoring their messy trays and plates on the table. I remained still and Megan kept eating. Jen turned to Megan and asked, "Are you coming?"

"No, you go ahead. I'm fine being late," Megan said. Pat looked at me and motioned that it was time to go.

"Go ahead," I told him. "I'll catch up."

It was just Megan and I. We inched over to the center of the table closing the space between us.

"Hi," she said, quiet and coy. She had long brown hair. It was often soaked in product, done-up to be wavy and shiny in appearance but oddly firm to the touch. Megan suffered from acne more than anyone else in seventh grade and wore braces. Her big blue eyes were two gems nestled in the mess of her growing body. She would be beautiful one day. I was nervous around her. She was my ally and she also controlled my future. She was my bridge to Jen and the gatekeeper too. We sat awkwardly for a few moments. A warm, discomforting feeling gelled in my stomach. I was too afraid to ask her and I believe she sensed my hesitation. Perhaps she wanted to watch me toil there in my seat, desperate to hear her voice. This was her moment of power. Finally, she spoke. "Jen wants to see you again." I waited for the final affirmation.

"After French class on Friday. Same place," she said.

"Thank you."

"Sure, it's fine."

"Does she really like me?"

"Yes, I think so."

"Do you think we can like be together?"

"I don't know. You'll have to wait."

Megan pushed aside her tray. "It's late," she said. "We'll get in trouble if we don't go."

I tried to remain cool though I was unhinged by her responses. Why couldn't Jen and I go out together properly, boyfriend and girlfriend? Beneath my shell I had been teetering, awaiting Megan's short dispatch since I had arrived at school that morning. I had waded through meaningless classes just to see her at lunch, to hear about the next phase of my relationship with Jen. Megan got up, gathered her things and began to head out. I stood up from the table and took my tray over to the tray holder. I emptied my half-eaten food into the disposal and walked back to the table. Megan was already to the door. She smiled at me as she left and repeated herself, once more as if I had forgotten her instructions.

"Friday, after French. The same place."

↓

Though there were students from across the world at the American School, actual Black people – American, African, or otherwise – were scarce. In the seventh grade there was another Black student, a girl named Lucretia also from the States. That made two of us in one class. We were a peculiarity like foreign exchange students flown into France from the edges of the world. In the first weeks of school Lucretia and I gravitated toward each other. She was funny and outspoken. She wore her dark brown hair in a ponytail and we traded rap tapes—from the gangster fantasies of N.W.A. to the dense, militant drill of Public Enemy. At lunch she found me and we talked in between classes.

Long before my obsession with Jen, Megan had approached me to find out if I liked any girls. She played matchmaker. I couldn't tell her my true response which was to say, "I am into almost all of them." Instead, I asked Megan, "Who should I like?" to which Megan replied, "Well isn't it obvious?"

"No," I said.

"Lucretia," she said. "You guys would be perfect together."

I was silent for a moment. Lucretia was my friend and beautiful and I don't know why I paused at the inquiry. Perhaps some calculation on what it would mean to be even tighter with my only Black crew at the school. Would we be stronger or more alone than before?

I was going to speak, but Megan had dropped the subject before I could respond.

"Don't worry about it," she said. "We'll keep working on it."

At home, I lay awake in bed for several nights attempting to understand what had happened to me. Megan's inquiry had implied something startling: Lucretia and I—we were both Black in a vast White space and thus the match was inevitable. In denying this union, I would be refuting the natural order of things. I would be a heretic. I thought of my parents. They were both Black. I thought of my friends' parents. They were all the same color. I was betraying a code, this much I knew.

Lucretia and I didn't talk as much after my conversation with Megan. We still had fun together, though we didn't see each other as much. At lunch she appeared less frequently at my table. She didn't seek me out during breaks from class. I understood then that the words— or lack thereof—I shared with Megan were public statements and that, quite possibly, it hadn't been Megan's idea to pair me, but perhaps Lucretia's idea instead. A cramp of disappointment clenched around my soul. Why had I betrayed that code? Was I following the actual desires of my nascent heart or succumbing to some implanted ideal of what we consider beautiful? My debt was severe. I had unwittingly driven a wedge between myself and my closest ally, further cloistering us away from each other in the immense Whiteness of our surroundings. At that young age we cannot always find the words, but we can feel the discomfort; and it felt like a hole I had fallen into—no doors, no signs, only the descent.

↓

I met Jen, for the second time in our secret place after French class. She was wearing white cutoff shorts with black leggings and a pair of white Chuck's. She smiled at me as I walked toward her under the stairs. She pulled me by the collar of my Britches rugby shirt and instinctively I grabbed her by the hair. My mouth toppled over her lips and her tongue shot out like a stone leaving a slingshot. I closed my eyes and ran my hands along her body – bony and firm. We shifted our heads and my mind unhinged itself from the stop-start motions of reality. The encounter seemed like fantasy – to have a woman in my arms, our mouths tied together like twine knots and my crotch firmly pressed against her body. We were only kissing, I knew this consciously, but it felt like intimacy beyond compromise. I opened my eyes to spy on Jen, to glimpse the posture of her face and, to my surprise, her eyes were open too. She had been watching me as my understanding of kissing, sex, and life unraveled. She laughed a little. She had caught me catching her. I closed my eyes again, remembering that I was supposed to enjoy this encounter, to not let my amazement and philosophical musings derail the most important fact of the situation: that it was actually happening. About a minute later she backed away from me, her lips coated with a glaze of saliva. It was over, the most revelatory moment of my week, perhaps my year. Jen took her things and left the building. I stood there, horny and deflated.

Back on the bus. Kristofor and the Clash. Combat rock. The casbah. Should I stay or should I go now? The boys talked about porn and Lucky Strikes. I held onto the knowledge of my unknown romance. Megan had told me that I couldn't tell anyone. The relationship was a secret. I couldn't understand why Jen didn't want anyone to know. Yet, I had no choice. I had to go along with it. The bus carried us away from the American school on the outskirts of the city and into the heart of the clamorous, infested thrill of Paris.

↓

I sat on my bed hunched over the small keyboard. It was a Casio MT-520. My parents had given it to me for Christmas. It had very small keys. The whole keyboard was about two-and-a-half feet long. Four octaves. There was a drum pad with very basic percussion sounds: kick, snare, hi-hat, conga, rim-shot. It had a small bank of beats it could play: Rock, Samba, Swing. There was a record function so I could play a beat and then record a keyboard part on top of it. The keyboard tones were limited: a piano that didn't sound like a real piano, a guitar that sounded like a thin piece of wire being plucked, and a tone simply called "synthesizer" that was piercing and sinister like a chainsaw cutting into a tree. It was a rudimentary instrument. Though, if the keyboard didn't offer much nor did I. My parents had insisted on a string of piano lessons. My teacher was an American expatriate who played jazz piano. He said he had come to Paris because the people cared about jazz in France. He spent an afternoon each week giving me lessons that I did not practice for. I much preferred the buzzing, raw sounds of the Casio than learning the 1-2-3-1-2 pattern of "Take Five".

I pressed the play button and listened to the loop of the basic drum pattern that echoed out of the thin speakers on either edge of the Casio. The drums didn't sound like the live drums on the Zeppelin tapes I had stolen from Georgia. They sounded almost clipped or compressed like the beats on rap albums—electronic and sparse. I let the beat play over and over; it was a basic rock beat, just a snare and a kick. I pushed a slider and brought in a hi-hat. I pushed another slider and brought in the conga. I didn't like the conga so I pulled it back. The simple beat bumped around the small confines of my room. I started playing a simple repetitive line on the keyboard, an eerie four-note run, like the theme from a horror film. I pressed the record button on the keyboard and captured the beat and keyboard line.

At the edge of my bed I had a notebook. Inside, I had scribbled several pages of rap lyrics, short verses of made-up adventures around Paris: hopping metro turnstiles, getting laid, and beating up French kids. I pulled the notebook close to the keyboard and I also grabbed my hand-held cassette recorder. I put a blank tape into the recorder and pressed play, letting it roll for a few seconds. I set it down on my bed near one of the keyboard speakers. I pushed the record button and then I pushed the play button on the keyboard. The low-budget beat and keyboard line spat out of the speakers. I let it roll for a couple of measures and then started rapping some lyrics from the notebook. I fumbled over some words and pressed stop on everything. I rewound the tape recorder. I pressed play on the keyboard, this time practicing the verse without recording. I tried this a few times before turning the tape recorder back on. When I practiced it was easy. With the recorder on, the tape rolling, I became nervous. I was acutely aware of the act of capturing my voice, of encasing the moment. The tape was rolling. I pressed play on the keyboard. The beat kicked in. Two measures, then I spat out the verse. No mistakes. It was done. I rewound the tape and listened to the product. The beat called out like muted drums in the basement of a house and the tinny tone of the synthesizer line cut above everything else in the mix. Then my voice dropped in, nasal and creepy. I was taken aback. Did I sound like that when I talked to people? The voice on the tape seemed so different than the way I imagined myself.

There was a knock at my door and my mother called my name. I stopped the tape and turned off the keyboard. My mom walked in and asked what I was doing. I felt oddly exposed, almost embarrassed.

"Nothing," I said.

"OK, I was just checking on you to make sure you were still alive back here."

She looked around my small room, briefly assessing what I had been up to. She didn't seem concerned. A teenager playing around with his keyboard on a Saturday afternoon was normal enough. My dad, though, wouldn't have seen the sense in it. To him, I should have been reading or studying math. "You should come up to the living room with me and your dad," my mom said.

I put aside my crude recording materials and walked up to the living room in our three-bedroom apartment and sat with my parents. On the weekends, their only time of freedom, they listened to jazz and classical in the living room and read books.

Our living room windows looked onto Rue de la Federation across from the beautiful Champ de Mars. There was a piano in the corner of our living room. It was the piano I never practiced on for my lessons but would try to play it along to rock albums when my parents were out of the apartment. My mom said Paris was a place of culture and that many Black artists had come here to express themselves outside of the oppression of the United States. She repeatedly mentioned the names James Baldwin and Richard Wright as if they were saints who had endured unspeakable tribulations. She said I was lucky to be in the place where such important Black Americans had been before me. I looked at my dad's CDs. He had a big collection of jazz and blues albums. There was one called *Basie Jam: Live at Montreaux '77* with Count Basie's smiling face, gray hairs and white teeth, gracing the cover. There was another called *Jam 2* with Basie and a large group of musicians posing for the cover. On the back cover the songs were listed, titles like "Mama Don't Wear No Drawers" and "Doggin' Around". The tracks were long swing anthems, most of them over ten minutes. I liked Jam 2 because there was a guitarist in the ensemble. That instrument seemed like the connection between my parents' music and the fuzzy rock I listened to. They hated my fondness of rap. I had to seek it out in secret. On MTV Europe I watched the epic videos of Guns n' Roses and then spotted that band's guitarist Slash in a new Lenny Kravitz video, a song called "Always on the Run". When I watched the video, little waves of energy flowed through my veins. I could feel a swell from my gut rising up through my chest and settling at the back of my throat. Shot on grainy black-and-white, Kravitz looked both vintage and modern on the screen. His tight-fitting clothes, the rings on his fingers and his long, wild dreadlocks were hippie signifiers but his coarse, soulful singing was immediate. He gripped the microphone tightly and roared through the verses. A Les Paul hung below his waist and he held its neck with one of his hands. The groove was funky, rooted in a grubby, repetitive guitar riff and punctuated by determined punches on the bass guitar. A rock band played behind Kravitz in the shadows and a two-piece horn section lurked off to the side. Slash stood stage-right of Kravtiz, his head pointed down and his massive, curly hair obscuring his face as he worked away on his own Les Paul. He was shirtless. Kravitz remained the unshakeable focus of the video, alternating between his intense delivery and periodic strums on the guitar. After the second verse, he called out Slash's name, like a bandleader, and Slash delved into a solo. But the focus returned to Kravitz as he took on the third verse. This was his domain. He was Black, he was a man, and he was rock n' roll all at once. My mom watched me watching this video on television. "You know that Slash is Black? They won't tell you that on MTV, but he's Black." How the hell did she know that, I wondered. Nonetheless, she was my mother and so I knew to believe her.

"They always want to take credit," she said. "White people taking rock n' roll. I like that Kravitz. He's Black. He represents us."

↓

The joints of the metro car rattled like loose bolts in a tin can as it rolled over the bridge. Below me, the Seine flowed by, the sight-seeing barges and their tourists inching lazily along the river. Across the Seine, the Eiffel Tower stood tall and imposing, its grand metallic phallus impossible to ignore, if only briefly, no matter how many times I rode by it on the 6 line toward Charles de Gaulle Etoile. It was a Saturday afternoon and I had escaped from my parents and from the encroaching walls of our apartment. I got off at Passy. I left the station and walked briskly to Pat's apartment. Intricately detailed stone apartment buildings surrounded me. I took their beauty for granted. Electric guitars buzzed sharply into my eardrums: the gloomy din of "Dazed and Confused", the lofty riffs of "How Many More Times?" or the slow blues of "I Can't Quit You Baby." *Led Zeppelin I* lived inside my Walkman. It was my fuel. I played it over and over, flipping the tape from side to side trying to recreate the waves of excitement I had experienced since hearing those songs for the first time. Occasionally, other tapes made their way into the Walkman but for this obsessive period *Led Zeppelin I* reigned, periodically substituted with the later Zeppelin tape, *Presence*. Every week at school Georgia would ask me, "Those tapes broke yet?"

I pressed the buzzer on the door to Pat's apartment building. His quiet voice and slow phrases rumbled lightly over the intercom. "Hello? Hello? Is that you?"

"Yes, man, let me in."

We huddled quietly around Pat's bed. He had blond hair, cut short, and freckles dotted his pale skin. He was about as tall as me, maybe 5' 8", and he had a long nose that ended in a sharp point. He was usually quiet but not shy. Up there, in his head, he concocted dirty jokes or insane fantasies of the girls in 7th grade. I understood him entirely. We were thirteen.

His apartment was beautiful and small. The floors and finishes around the doors and entryways were a dark hardwood. The large windows looked onto other apartments and the expanse of Paris. Most of my friends lived like this, in one neighborhood or another, in small yet gorgeous environs. Those who were outside of Paris, living off some stretch of the RER, often had grand, sprawling houses in the suburbs. They weren't like American suburbs where everything was plastic and new and the same. They were part of the lush countryside which, save for the cars and other modern amenities, looked as they had three hundred years before.

"These are cool," Pat said.

I had brought over copies of *Daredevil, the Man Without Fear*. Issues 182 – 184. The storyline was wild: the Punisher and the Daredevil separately hunting down drug dealers who were killing kids with angel dust. The Daredevil's alter ego was Matt Murdock, a blind lawyer who dedicated himself to defending the innocent and bringing underworld mob bosses to justice. The Punisher was Frank Castle, a cop whose family had been killed by gangsters. He had turned vigilante, swearing to eradicate all criminals from the face of the earth. The Punisher's path to justice was vengeance by execution. The Daredevil wanted to apprehend criminals and have them stand trial before his counterpart Matt Murdock. Like Georgia had lent me his Zeppelin tapes I would lend Pat my comics and I had to hammer him constantly to get them back. I preferred to come over to his place and watch him read the comics so that I could take them back home with me when he was done.

"So have you decided?" I asked.

He had recently told me in confidence that he had developed a crush on Jen. We had been absently throwing basketballs around the blacktop at school. He had just come out and said, "I really like Jen." I knew he was serious when he said it and my gut had seemed to swell with a dizzying toxin as he played out for me his quietly kept months-long longing for Jen. He told me everything, from the fantasies he had harbored during his classes to his isolated moments alone in his bedroom. I did my best to navigate him away from the possible dissolution of my own secret romance with Jen. I told him to think it over, to make sure he really liked her before we attempted to make it actually happen. Then he called me at home over the weekend and invited me to his apartment. I knew he had made his decision the second I heard his voice on the phone, but I played along and went over to his place.

"Yes," he said, "I definitely like Jen."

"This is good news," I said to Pat. "She isn't seeing anyone. I think we can make it happen."

Pat's eyes lit up. I knew what he wanted to ask me before he even said it. "So you'll talk to Megan?"

"Yeah, I'll talk to her on Monday."

He smiled and touched my shoulder. He thanked me and I told him not to thank me. "We are friends," I said. I told him to finish reading the issues of Daredevil so that I could take them back home with me, safe and secluded in the corners of my bedroom next to the Uncanny X-Men and my notebook of rap lyrics.

I met with Megan in a foyer between the middle school and high school. We often met there to discuss barters of romance between our fellow classmates. It was our bargaining ground, where I could make the case for myself or help out a friend. It was where I had first confessed to her that I liked Jen and where she had first told me that Jen would secretly begin meeting me after French class so that we could make out with each other. Now I was in the strange position of speaking on Pat's behalf. I told her bluntly that Pat was interested in Jen. She told me she would find out if it could work and that she would tell me the next day. We didn't say anything about Jen and me. I was too afraid to ask or to look like I actually cared. The next day, Megan met me again and told me that the very next day Jen wanted to meet Pat after school. She said that Jen was interested, "wanted to try it out." She didn't mention me at all as if, even when alone, we could not speak of the secret meetings. By phone, that night, Megan and I arranged a group meeting of students after school and from there Jen and Pat could take off alone and go talk. By the next morning it seemed that about half of the seventh grade knew about Jen and Pat's meeting after school. It was an event. Georgia asked me, "Are you going to the meeting after school?"

I held back my anxiety and told him cheerfully, "I can't wait."

We met in the center of the middle school, a group of fifteen or so, stalking the hallways telling jokes. First the boys kept to themselves while the girls trailed behind, all of us afraid to break the line between us. I walked with Pat and Georgia. We led the pack to the back corners of the middle school, ending up near the room where we had chorus practice. Jen abruptly pushed her way into our group, her bony arms wrapping around us as she edged in between me and Pat. "Hey fuckers," she said. "What are you guys talking about?"

"Nothing," we said. Pat looked at me, a fertile mix of excitement and fear brimming in his eyes. Georgia peeled off from us and sank back into the larger group. It was just the three of us walking ahead of everyone. Jen dropped her arm from my shoulder but her other arm stayed on Pat. He looked at me again, beaming like a silly, obedient dog. I knew it was time to let go, but I couldn't make myself fall back.

Jen turned to me and spoke crisply, "I want to talk to Pat about something. Give us a few minutes." I met her eyes and they were in equal parts hateful, inviting, and ambivalent. I didn't know what she thought of me or what she had ever thought of me. I was too stunned to even make a scene. I nodded like a diplomat. "Sure thing," I said. I turned around and walked toward the group, now ten or fifteen feet behind me. I must have looked like a fool, hanging on that long. But no one else knew except Megan who stood in the far back talking to some girls, ignoring me. Momentarily, I was neither important nor repulsive – I simply didn't exist.

Pat and Jen walked into a classroom together, across from the chorus room. They closed the door behind them. The boys and girls in our group hissed with glee. They ran to the outside of the classroom wall and pressed their cheeks and ears to it as if they could actually hear something. Someone told us to *shhh*, to not be so loud. Georgia, shorter than the rest of us, ran down the hall and came sauntering back with a chair. He climbed the chair and pulled himself up on the ledge where the wall ended and the classroom window began. He turned around and told us, "They aren't kissing, just talking." Half the group scurried through the hallway looking for chairs. I wouldn't have anything to do with it. They climbed their chairs and peaked over the wall, looking in on the couple. An excited boy dropped down from his chair and announced with an exasperated whisper, "They're kissing." Those who hadn't been on the chairs now pushed and pulled at their classmates to get down so they could get a look too. A boy looked down at me, calling out my name, urging me to come up and see. He was being generous giving up his spot on the chair so that I could have a look. I shook my head at first but he wouldn't let me be. Finally, I relented and climbed the chair. Peering over the wall and through the window into the classroom, I could see them sitting on chairs awkwardly turned toward each other kissing deeply, their heads shifting back and forth. The boys around me were moaning quietly in awe and the girls were oddly silent, neither for it nor against it. I dropped down to the floor and edged away from the wall. The hallway hummed with chatter. Megan looked at me now. At first she seemed interested in me as if she had wanted to know how all of this would affect me. Then she was almost sad, embarrassed to have been mean, her blue eyes aching with a confused, adolescent regret. She was always the nice one. I slipped away from the thrall, grabbed my belongings from my locker and walked out of the school. The afternoon bus had already left so I would have to take the city bus to the metro and get home on my own. I climbed the hill to the bus stop and put my headphones on. "How Many More Times", "I Can't Quit You Baby", "Communication Breakdown".

↓

My parents and I took a trip in their new Volvo sedan. We were driving to Germany, to the Ramstein army base to stock up on American goods. As much as my mother liked French breads and cheeses she felt it important to also have a healthy stock of Morton salt, Crisco cooking cream, and Lipton tea. She was born in Texas and we needed some roots in this foreign land. The drive was five hours. I spent the trip mostly in silence, parked in the backseat, always behind my mother because she was shorter than my dad and left me more legroom. I read comic books but sometimes I got car sick if I read for too long. We would pull over for a minute so that I could catch my breath. I would spend the rest of the trip with my head against the glass looking out the window at the European countryside. Mostly my parents played their tapes – jazz, blues and classical music. The blues I secretly liked, the jazz I could live with, and the classical I hated. Eventually, I would sink a tape into my Walkman and put on my headphones. I was listening to my *Led Zeppelin I* tape when my father called out my name. I heard him calling me but I ignored him and kept looking out the window. He turned around, looking at me and called again. I slipped off the headphones.

"That music is too loud."

"Sorry."

"Why do you have to listen to it like that?"

"Because I need to drown out your music."

"You're going to blow out your ears."

"OK."

We were silent for a few moments as the car pushed forward. "You know," I said, "Maybe we could listen to my music for a little while on the stereo." My dad groaned.

"What are you listening to?" my mom asked, "Your Led Zeppelin tape?"

"Yeah."

"Well I guess we could listen to a few songs," she said. My dad let out an indignant grunt.

"Not on this stereo..."

My mom looked at him and he quietly relented, focusing his eyes on the road. I took the tape out of my Walkman and passed it to my mother. She eyed the white cassette for a moment before pushing it into the tape player. I told her to rewind it to the beginning of the side. As it started to play a mix of excitement and anxiety rushed through me. The church organ introduction of "Your Time Is Gonna Come" bubbled up from the speakers. The song's back-porch acoustic guitars echoed gently enough through the car as not to erupt a concerned reaction from my parents. I eased into my seat thankful that the next song, "Black Mountain Side", was an acoustic guitar instrumental though I was acutely aware of the piercing electric guitars in "Communication Breakdown" that immediately followed it. As the sharp, distorted guitar solo ripped through the center of "Communication Breakdown" my father didn't say anything, he just turned down the volume. A touch of regret tugged at my stomach. What had come over me? What experiment was I seeking to play out? It was clear: my parents didn't like this music. It was better off in my headphones. I relaxed a bit as the song ended. Robert Plant's gravelly voice announced the next song with a long moan. He sang the line, "Oh, I can't quit you baby," and the band dropped in with its taut, focused blues. I felt relieved. I knew the blues song would bridge the awkward gap between me and my parents. My father turned up the volume a bit and the first verse unfolded in what seemed to be a comfortable silence in the car. We pushed on, quietly, along the highway towards the air force base.

And then, my father – his voice like an alarm – broke the harmony of the moment. "What is this?" he asked.

"What?" I replied.

"What is this? This isn't theirs. They stole this."

His sudden shift in attitude felt like an attack. I lunged forward from my seat, leaning closer to the front where my parents sat. "What do you mean?" I said. "What do you mean they stole this? This is their song."

"No," my father said, his voice increasingly more agitated. It sounded like he was the one who was under attack, as if my firm denial had offended him, as if my words had pressed deeply into his skin, punctured his flesh and opened fresh some old, forgotten wounds. "No, this is not theirs. This is an old blues song. It was written long before they came around. And don't tell me I'm wrong. I know my music when I hear it."

Guitar lines crackled around us, a raw solo emanating from the speakers. I sat back in my seat confused and annoyed. My father was facing the road, frowning. That frown, his look of dissatisfaction, was unsettling. It made his eyes, his whole face seem like it was alive with anger and disappointment. I felt like I had done something wrong. My throat clenched and words did not come easily from my mouth but I forced myself to speak. "I am sorry. I didn't know."

My mother turned around to look at me and when she spoke her voice was calm and instructive as if she were giving me important advice that I would use for the rest of my life. "White people are always taking Black music," she said. "And they never give credit. Elvis, the Rolling Stones. It's all around us. And no one ever says anything. So, you need to know what you're listening to. You need to know where it came from."

I was looking out the window, my face flush with anger, embarrassment, and disbelief. "OK," I said. "Just give me my tape."

My father ejected the tape from the stereo and handed it to me. I put it aside on the seat. He wasn't frowning anymore. He looked ahead to the road. The anger had passed. He spoke aloud and though I knew he was talking to me it seemed more like he was making an announcement to the world at-large. "The blues, son, it's our music. You need to know that." I looked at him briefly then returned my gaze to the window, the European countryside shimmying by us at a quickening pace. We rolled toward the air force base. We rode in silence.

↓

Pat and Jen were a couple. Everyone thought it was cute. Megan surprised me when she pulled me aside at school one day and told me that my secret meetings with Jen weren't over. She gave me the familiar instructions: after French class, under the stairs. I met Jen there and we embraced each other as we had done before. This time she spoke. She said, "We're being bad."

She smiled as she said it and then we made out. Then she was gone. I was back on the bus, Joe Strummer and Mick Jones' thunderous guitars exploding around my ears, Kristofer talking about his homeland. The dense park called Bois de Boulonge swept by us as the bus pushed deeper into the city. They said that prostitutes roamed the park at night, that you could do anything you dreamed of if you had five-hundred francs. They said there were women who turned into men and men who turned into women. They said Magic Johnson of the L.A. Lakers had caught HIV from a girl he had met in the park. I met Jen the next week under the stairs after French class. It was a bad kiss. Her mouth felt cold. (Did she think my mouth was cold too?) It was still better than being alone but something essential had left us. She and Pat were a proper boyfriend and girlfriend now. After we kissed, she wiped her mouth, looked at me and laughed before running away to her bus. I had lost her. Pat invited me to go to a movie with them over the weekend but I declined. I hovered around our apartment chewing on baguette, making rap beats on my keyboard and reading comic books. In a feverishly engrossing storyline, the Daredevil's arch-nemesis, the Kingpin, had ruined him, got him strung-out on heroin causing him to lose his legal practice. Matt Murdock was living on the streets, a blind, disgraced lawyer and superhero fallen from grace.

I met Megan in the foyer after school. She was tense. She knew what I wanted and knew she couldn't give it to me. "I don't want it to be over," I said.

"Well, I'm sorry, it is."

"But I was here first. It should be me, not Pat."

"But it's not."

"Why were we a secret?" I asked.

"Because that's how she wanted it."

"But I wanted to go out with her."

"I'm sorry," Megan said. She reached out for me but I was so angry I didn't let her touch me.

"I want to date her. Can't you ask her to go with me instead?"

"No," she said. "Don't you understand? She and Pat are public. Boyfriend and girlfriend. She can't date you."

I wanted to argue, to offer some possibility of reclaiming my lost crush. I was shocked and hurt. I cowered away from Megan, almost unable to look at her or think about my sorry self. In a wild instant she turned and snapped at me.

"Stop looking so sad!" she said. "You got what you wanted. Everyone gets what they want. But no one ever asks about me. I am lonely. I want someone to kiss but no one ever asks." I looked at her eyes, tucked in behind her tacky hair and marked face. I felt sick and embarrassed for myself. I stepped away from her. I hadn't realized her pain.

"I am sorry," I said.

"It's okay."

"Do you want a hug?" I asked. It was all I could think of.

She looked up at me with her beautiful eyes. I tried to imagine for a moment being her boyfriend—kissing in empty classrooms and holding hands at lunch—but I couldn't make it stick, even in my imagination. She wrapped her arms around me. I squeezed her tightly trying my best to mean it. We stood there for a few moments, embracing each other but oddly apart from everything we really wanted.

Pat and Jen broke up a month or so later. She liked someone new. Everyone had lost except Jen. The news made me uneasy. I felt awful for Pat, awful for what I had done behind his back. I talked to him at school but didn't call him on the weekends. I hid away, hoping to disappear. I was now all alone. I had used and been used. And I knew—just knew inside—that Lucretia wouldn't have led me to this empty place. And I also knew I had made every decision, chosen my own way.

Pat called me on a weekend afternoon. I was at home listening to music, reading comic books. "Let's go down to the park," he said.

"Sure thing," I said. I couldn't avoid him forever.

I met him across the street from my house. We walked down the Champ de Mars toward the Eiffel Tower. Tourists were zipping about frantically. Every entrance to the tower – the stairs, the elevator – was jammed up with a long, winding line. Merchants sold meaningless knick-knacks – little tower replicas, gaudy t-shirts, and cheap, plastic toy helicopters that flew around in the air for about three seconds before nose-diving to the ground. The tourists bought the knick-knacks. Even I had a miniature Eiffel Tower keychain my mother had given me. We pushed past the tower, right up to the Seine. We looked over the bridge to the Trocadero. Down below, tourist barges floated by on the river. Food trucks sold skinny, French hot dogs and cans of Coke. We bought some Cokes. We walked down the steps at the edge of the bridge and sat down on a stone curb right by the Seine.

"Are you doing OK?" I asked.

"Yeah, I can't complain." Pat said.

He turned to me and looked at me with his mild eyes. "I know about you and Jen. About what was happening after French class."

I turned away from him. "I am sorry about that. I really am. I just got too into her. I should have told you..."

"Don't worry about it," he said. "I forgive you." We sat in silence for a while. The barges inched by. Tourists had their cameras out. They were wearing their big sunglasses and white shorts. I stewed in the realization of my selfishness and betrayal. Pat wasn't a silly dog. He was kind. I was an idiot. He spoke up, "Things are weird with girls."

"Yeah."

"Let's get out of here."

We got up and started to walk away. "You owe me." he said. "I want that new Daredevil series. Bring it to school next week. This isn't a loan, it's a gift."

It didn't matter – he always kept all of my comic books anyway, just like I kept Georgia's tapes.

"Sure," I said. "That seems fair."

We walked away, the buzz of tourism echoing all around us. With their cameras, their maps, and their tour guides – they were all trying to capture something: a memory, a keepsake, or a piece of knowledge to take home from Paris. Being here was important. It was a milestone, something to aspire to. But we were ignorant, possessed by crushes, comic books, and music. Everything else was just noise.

Suzanne Buffam

Baby On Board

The baby is blameless, I can't argue with that. She hasn't told a single lie in her life, let alone cheated, however inadvertently, on her taxes, failed to properly dispose of toxic paint, padded a year-end report, spat up red wine all over a vintage mohair blanket in an old friend's parents' ski lodge on New Year's Eve and then shoved it under the couch without mentioning it to anyone, or flicked a candy wrapper out the window of a Subaru stuck in traffic while pretending to adjust the side-view mirror. Her conscience, if a baby can be said to have a conscience at all, is infinitely clearer than any middle-aged woman's, I grant. On the other hand, most middle-aged women I know have done at least some good in the world so far and may well be in the process of doing more at this moment – harvesting stem cells, for example, or campaigning for bail reform, or bringing a class-action lawsuit against a multinational petroleum conglomerate, teaching refugees, feeding honeybees, or even just sitting in traffic on the expressway *en route* to a Mommy-and-Me Kindermusik class across town – whereas baby, so feeble she can't even buckle up the harness on her own crusty car seat – craps in her sleep and wakes screaming. In some cultures, a baby isn't even given a name until her fifth birthday, I once read. It is the elders, in those cultures, whose safe passage on the journey must above all be ensured, and baby who must earn her seat of honor on board.

No Warning

The newly-appointed program director, whose prior career in the British mental health system had amply equipped him for all manner of dispute, promptly informed the assembled members of the English faculty, who'd been debating the precise wording on their syllabi for months, that content warnings, as such, were based on a *fundamental misunderstanding* of the way trauma works. "A trigger is as likely to be a smell," he pointed out.

Bold Statements

When the famous aging editor tells the young writer that as wise and clever as she is, she is not prepared to be flagrant, she feels that he has seen the true timid nature of her soul and is ashamed. But the edits he suggests are so flagrant that she wonders if he even means for her to apply them, or if, by urging her to make a "bold statement," he is merely attempting to make a bold statement himself.

Hard Numbers (Easy Math)

I once knew a man who was convinced he wouldn't live past fifty-six. Fifty-six, at twenty-three, seemed fair enough to him. Keats, he pointed out, didn't live past twenty-five. Yesterday I learned this man is still alive, somewhere on the far side of the country with a young wife and twins, teaching high school English behind a bushy greying beard. Is he still writing that masterpiece? He's got four years.

Anaïs Duplain

My Phone Will Be Off

Your fucking bulshit. So that when I hear it—

I know what it *sound like*. If my feeling wasn't   right, now.
    An open small.   Cross over.   The extremes:
                                as if I have allowed myself to be mistaken
        for the sake of awakening, for crossing over.   Thank god
I can walk away.   Outright, damned,
                                    contemplative.   This isn't a
decision
we make together.   We work up into this choice.

It hurt and is over.   It's finally over, king.   Exhausted
                    by itself, by way of revelation.   Geographic distance,
        finery, spastic emotion,   a Lyft ride for a friend
    I paid for, distraction, sleep.   A recombobulation.

        This a phrase meant to get us   to another one,
a malaise meant to get us   into another conversation.   Balance
        settles wherever it's going to.   We find a balance
point when we're in it; it finds us   when we're there.
The Socratic method   leads to a heart of darkness. The Socratic method.
        A poetry we learn   to forgive. If I take serious
my feeling. Time to feel, now.   This may bring us
to rework what we've had.   Maybe thoroughly destroyed,
the settlement.   And I've succeeded, too, because of it.
                    The ability to withstand pain.   If I lead you   to a hole,
                                where's precision take place at?

Claire Donato

A Story about a Naked Girl in a Snow Globe on the Shelf of an American Multinational Retail Corporation

A girl is sitting in a snow globe on the shelf of an American multinational retail corporation. She is naked, and a man re-stocking the shelf with various other snow globes of divergent shapes, colors, sizes and styles is studying her body with his penis in lieu of completing his work. He is inspecting the girl to see how naked she is, and to discern whether or not she is naked enough to hold in mind when she doesn't exist in plain sight. For this man does not possess the ability to engage in object permanence with the women who inhabit his life: his mother, his daughter, his wife. It always seems as if they're there when they're there, and that, when they're gone, he's completely alone: at peace, at long last—and empty, sans women whose needs and desires only serve as distractions.

The girl in the snow globe is also alone, and also empty, and also pornography—she is naked, after all, and was rendered by a 58-year old factory worker who compulsively masturbated as he hand-painted her breasts—but because she is enclosed in water in a transparent sphere punctuated by white particles that fall through the water when the globe is shaken, her aloneness induces within her the sorts of existential quandaries typically reserved for a first-year undergraduate composition course. For example, *Recount a time when you faced a challenge, setback, or failure. How did it affect you, and what did you learn from the experience? Or, Describe a topic, idea, or concept you find so engaging it makes you lose all track of time. Why does it captivate you? What or who do you turn to when you want to learn more?*

One can see through glass but not water, nor can one not see through water. The snow globe's water doesn't have a color, so something about it feels transparent, or the fluorescent lights of the American multinational retail corporation make it such that when the man who is studying the girl's body with his penis re-stocks the the shelf while looking at the girl, she can't discern whether or not he's a ghost. He is a pervert and she resents him, but she is also in love with him because he is the only man in the store who continuously returns to the snow globe aisle, and it would be fatal to fall in love with anyone who merely browses the snow globes, for those visitors to the aisle rarely return. Take, for instance, the man dressed in a camouflage vest who fingered her snow globe's glass on Christmas Day (the American multinational retail corporation is open on Christmas Day; everything without a heart is)—when this man arrived, she became enamored with the whorls and lines of his fingers, which stained the glass within which she resides, and in her enamored state, she thought about entwining her small fingers with his big ones, and experienced this scale of size as erotic, and experienced too a fantasy of breaking through her snow globe's glass to find a ring for his finger in the American multinational retail corporation's jewelry department, but in this fantasy she had no idea how to 1) scale the ring counter to view the ring collection; 2) extract the ring from its case; 3) carry the ring to a secure location containing the man whose name she does not know; and 4) speak, and therefore propose. By the time she had crystallized this fantasy in her mind, the man was gone, and she missed him, but she could not cry in the snow globe because a girl in a snow globe is already contained by water, and tears are also water, thus there is no differentiating them from the snow globe's interior, nor can one distinguish the snow globe from the ocean, where she is glued to the floor and can't move her arms or legs, her hands or feet.

Frog and Toad and Termination

There is a frog
and there is a toad
and there is a snail
delivering a letter

There is a girl
and there is a snail
and there is a home
that cannot be defined
by placelessness and void

There is an apartment
and there is a home office
where there is a cat
on the desk
eating its supper

The apartment
that is a home
no longer
exists

due to the
walls
surrounding it

The new home
is not a
home — nor

is it a sanctuary
where

There
is a hermit
and there is a tag
and on this tag
is emblazoned
a slogan
that cannot
define *us*

Us, in fact, is
our home
we took away
when we saw
it occupied
a destination

But the girl is not
me, and the home
is not thee, and
the snail is slow,
and I am not

one
or
other:

I am both.

The Hopeless Case

Emily says Claire says neither human is a turtle.
Every turtle is human and has therefore made mistakes.
Claire stands against a wall with a plate pressed to her face.
Emily carries Claire inside her shell atop her back.
She writes Claire's errors down, and Claire's errors are the case.
Now one turtle (Claire) is feeling quite exhausted with herself!
And the other turtle (Emily) is accustomed to not knowing.
The third is sick of hearing about it: Emily
at rest on the chair with socks on her feet; Claire
lying on her back, smearing language on the ceiling.
Emily asks: Is there a way we can interpret what that means?
After which Claire describes a turtle getting drunk.
Depressing, Emily says.
I feel in love, Claire says. Is there any hope?
Hope is the only thing, says Emily.

Harper Quinn

It Was Summer

and we all had our own watermelon
to carry over the threshold.

In the exploded diagram
of the mechanical bull

I was sitting
at the kitchen table

balancing my checkbook,
harmonizing my debts & assets.

Where there's an orchid
there's the orchid's dirt.

The Dankness

The proof.
The pudding.
The waft of the dried-up
shard of soap.

The rip in the spider's well-tuned web?
The dankness
under the rock!

Since when had I started
sparing myself the details
that I loved so dearly?

Not even a newt
gets to stay an eft forever

Joel Craig

Off the Shoulder of Orion

So this is starlight
finally
I can see it
clearly
but why
can't I remember
what is
the word
for always
being
aware
of which specific
emotion
is churning
inside of you
until you can't
imagine
what is the word
for being
brave
for having
a brave
face
if I'd ever
had a first
drink I'd
have liked
something
sweeter
a Dark
and Stormy

maybe
but words
can be cheap
or forgotten
like so many
moments in life
what I see
is what I get
down on paper
so paper
can be folded
up and left
in a pocket
lost
in the wash
we used
to say
but to whom
are we speaking
who are we
staring at
exactly
the life
being lived
outside
this unthinkable
window
is moving
too fast
through
a gradient
color
field
and which day
is it
anyway
a birthday
or a solstice

I can't always
get the right
words out
but still
they're spilling
onto the page
with purpose
this opening up
looks
so good
in pictures
the bed
is everywhere
covered
in soft
linens
I could lay
down in
this grass
forever
but what exactly
happens
as you climb
right up
to the edge
of the volcano
and look
down
to see
there it is
your reflection
I'm so glad
you're here
to share this
you say
backing into
your heart
memory

how do you
know
which beam
of light
is moving
faster
you know what
would be good
right now
is a bowl
of beans
and cornbread
it's funny
sometimes
what you love
most
is also
exactly
what you need
the word
for what
you most
need
this wealth
of arguments
in the beginning
feels
like work
if you see me
standing
in the window
throw a stone
I'm looking
for the right
attention
to give
and I want
to know

when
you are
at present
all we need
is a glimmer
of awareness
in this night
sky
I'll take it
over this pile
of tubes
and wires
any day
what is
the word for
who
do you love
dearly
but can't
imagine
the word
for being
tangled up
inside
sometimes
the words
spill
right out
and if
you're lucky
you can
catch up
with lightning
otherwise
it's complete
darkness
—your poetry
is so dark

poetry
should rhyme
why can't you
write something
happy—
and I'd say
mother
everyone
sees starlight
differently
but still
they call it
starlight
I don't know
what poetry
she actually
read
my father's
maybe
a limerick
or Christian
hard
-rhyming
ballad maybe
Reader's Digest
in the waiting room
or New Yorker
blank verse
where someone goes
to a dog park
and has this
big epiphany
about—
what
is a dog park
she cuts in
because
some part of her

has always lived
in a century
I've never
been to
what is
an epiphany
I wave to her
in return
for what
is the word
for who
is rescuing
whom
what is the pill
for just being
subterranean
on another planet
because emptiness
and loneliness
are different
territories
where the brain
can be truly
righteously
on fire
and it's okay
to say
we can
love you
even burning
off the shoulder
of Orion
what is
the word
for this sky
is so bright
and here
we linger

in the afterglow
the rest of us
so sensibly
not quite
together
waiting
for help
to arrive

CL Young

Introduction

A woman for whom I have a fear of admiration started it.
Light a fire, then light another fire.
I grew up wanting to know myself.
I grew up understanding my assignment: know yourself.
I suggest that I might be someone born with a loss already lost.
The friends listen, nod vigorously.
In the car at the conclusion of the discussion after the discussion.
The condition is just right for us to catch on each other.
All the practice I've been doing waiting for you.
Breaking into houses through bedroom windows.
The songs we hear are not old enough to be called old.
I choose one on a jukebox.
That plays only after we leave.
Instead of moving out, I eat dinner.
I try to dream of my teacher.
For learning that cannot come in daylight or in person.
Root system visible outside the ground.
I've written a poem one way a thousand times.
I've written the same poem a hundred lines a different way.
A file cabinet full of love letters.
It was suggested that I write about Helen.
An essay not on learning to be beautiful but *how*.
Nobody likes to admit that it gets a little more okay if we use the right substances.
To create conditions in which there is something to notice.
The sex inside the wall.
I had the feeling our legs were scratching marks into the floor.
At a house on the coast of the Pacific Ocean.
I sat with my back leaning against the kitchen.
It felt like before even as it happened.
I spun all around trying to sort out who to love.
Many pictures were taken of my spinning.

The caption said: Learning.

Sprinklers going off at all hours of the morning and night.

Water on the sidewalks and on cars.

It's never felt more like the end of the world.

A letter written in California and sent from Seattle page 21 of a book.

My body from above moving from one place to another.

If I were better at drawing would be a good map.

That in youth we promise never to believe.

Those things we later come to believe.

How later the letters went bad.

In the way only letters can do.

Arriving with nothing really to say.

When the hole is as deep as it goes and all around is dirt.

I want a room in my mind with a door that closes.

In an altered state in the middle of the Olympic Peninsula I convince myself.

Not only to continue into my happiness but to think of others while I masturbate.

I allow the dead in.

It's not about getting young again or even the future.

Boise to Seattle.

Los Angeles to Portland.

Seattle to Boise.

Boise to Portland.

Portland to Colorado.

Colorado to Idaho.

I'd like most to be what moves across an Etch A Sketch to make it look like anything.

My hair was long and blonde before it was gone.

The paper I picked from the oracle was blank.

Beauty is as beauty does.

When you come across something and choose to make it yours.

It is important to let go of something else.

And something else.

A book cut by hand and sewn together.

Sometimes I look inside people by accident.

I look out everywhere for wings flapping.

Phone calls every couple of weeks to remember who's here.

This is an ordinary story.

That I can say I love you.

And then we part like it's Sunday and there's school tomorrow.
There was a time I fucked everything I could that would teach me.
A poet said: "I wish you could say multiple things at the exact same time."
A photograph of an arctic desert.
A report of what was happening in my life before I imagined living.
How I still woke up.
Now I wait for each morning to arrive so that I can see you unraveled.
The way your eyes opened once I thought you were a baby.
They looked at first overwhelmed by light.
Then they looked at me.
A person shouldn't know everything.
How to love someone who only thinks about death.
How to make what is sick in you about the person nearest.
Talk until what comes out of your mouth is true no matter what.
Stop answering the phone.
Let it turn September.
Let the plants dry out.
I thought there would be a sort of rectangle I could hand to anyone to make.
Whatever it was they needed.
A stack of notes waiting for the mail.
Hello.
How are you.
Thank you.
For not dying.
Because I can't seem to get any closer to what I'd rather give.
I walk a path back toward the war I was taught.
To call something else.
A sun rises anyway.
Mouth come on stop.
When you're asked to stop.

Yam Gong, translated by James Shea & Dorothy Tse

Reclamation

I don't recognize it anymore
this reclaimed land—when it was first filled in
my warm naked butt lazed there
under the afternoon sun for an entire summer!
Salt in the wind, charm of the sea
and youthful guts—
if someone tossed a coin from the ferry
you'd hear splashes in the waves
No one emerged until the coin was between his teeth
Resolved to be a wild stray,
I'd roam from sampan
to sampan
Back then, whenever night fell
the Flute King stood
on an outcropping in a spotted cloak
blowing a light into each
gloomy paraffin lamp
Then came Mr. Lively Ghost No. 7—
with an uncanny knack, he gripped a handsaw on his figure-four knee
drawing a nimble bow across
Zhou Xuan's songs, one after another
Wriggling into the most congested places
like a little mouse
under a sweaty armpit, under a piss-soaked crotch:
my bulging eyes saw a Northerner swallowing a large egg-shaped stone
(spitting it back up with blood)
A young boatman buying Spanish fly
A grizzled old man smashing bricks on his forehead
lashing each limb with a seven-sectioned whip

Then he'd rub on the tinctures that he hawks
Night after night—fifty cents cures a dozen pains,
ten cents for a piece of gum, chewed
forever, among the cymbals, gongs, and drums,
the laboring masses are all down-and-out scholars from an ancient story
brushing up against a street opera actress buying fruit candy
and so a life is ordinary and radiant
In those days I was young and "improper"
braving the rain just to hear some dirty jokes,
head trembling full of cryptic prophecies
and cryptic tales—*dried husks*
sinking and large stones bobbing
The endless waves never washed away the contest between Zhuge Liang
    and Liu Bowen
With looks of astonishment
we followed the storyteller's fan opening and closing
as he asked every bystander,
"Five hundred years ago, I knew about you—
whom in the future do you know today?"
(but no one ever asked him about Grimm or Andersen)
And so it was:
searching everywhere for a sword teacher
until one day like a bolt
out of the blue a great fire broke out
burning down the Red Lotus Temple and burning down
a three-story hotel across the street,
burning to death the Flute King in his speckled coat, the palm-reader,
the fortune teller, the psychic, and their fellow diviners,
Tiny Su from Shek Tong Tsui who sang Western songs,
that entire family of the Daoist shaman,
that entire family
No one was spared—
Only an auntie of the night
remained, still
standing by the seaside
Ah, this life
teaches her to believe
that she will be reunited in eighteen years

with a man
who has a familiar face
or an unfamiliar face

Mary Szybist

Aubade—

We were wandering a vast tundra

firestretching to the Arctic shore—

wandering through smoke rising

from peat and deep snow, moving

toward a black ocean but so

slowly I never felt closer to it.

On it goes. Good morning.

Yes, that's my hand stroking your neck

even if neither of us can feel it.

You were an arm's length away

when I looked up and saw it

wasn't you I'd taken with me into

the dream—even if you looked just like you.

Smoke exhaled us. We grew

thirstier. One of us

prayed. One of us said how

we're part of a mind that's changing

hundreds of times faster than in

any previous extinction. I didn't know,

in the tundra, when we were

walking, or when we had laid ourselves down.

We were trying to hear if there was anything

left to creep toward us. Anything

besides the fire. And when the moon

asked, we said yes,

like bread. We ate our ash like bread.

Nathaniel Mackey

"Who shoot 'im?" Mr. Foster asked.

"They shoot 'im," she said; "they shoot 'im like he was a bird."

"Who?" Mr. Foster insisted.

"The police," she said. "Some say 'twas the white inspector, an' others wus the ordinary police, but he dead."

"Where wus he?" Mr. Foster asked.

"In the tree," she said. "When the law declare they all run here, there an' everywhere, an' poor Po run up the tree. The police see him where he go, an' they aim all together at the top at the tree. An' they got 'im. My poor Po fall down like a bird."

—George Lamming, *In the Castle of My Skin*

All Eyes on the Athmic

—"mu" two hundred eighty-fifth part—

Albeit eyes were now of no use, all eyes
  were on the athmic. That we were witnessing
a sort of witchcraft occurred to us now, how
                                the
  birds could be back having never left. Was
    it that return was intrinsic to wing and feather,
  we wondered, a part of them being there. They
                                  were
  us and we were them, shot by cops at the foot
of a tree as though fallen from branches, bird lives
  no more mattering than ours. Hazmat athmicity
                                 it
    was, a way of turning away, obliquity a way
  we once put it, wrapped as we were in textile and

tendency, an opening-out ratcheting back... It
                                                    was
all in the realm of the torpedo prez, the appren-
    tice prez now the corona king. We carved a way
out for ourselves, à la Mosley. We heard wood's
                                                    inner
    life, its low whisper, a round sound, à la Mob-
ley, it turned out. Mosley and Mobley were steps up
    a hill, a wooden stair caught on their feet, a metal
                                                    one
        as well. Athmic trek it was, athmic trudge. The
    numbers were coming in, the postcomputational
        ones we carved our way with, gouge's decantation,
chisel, file... Scraper decantation held sway. I went
                                                    over,
        myself on the azimuth, the angle we took athmic-
    ity to be, the angle athmicity was, a cupped hand's dry
    run, a watering leaflessness. I wanted my head in
                                                    the
    clouds, arms at an angle, the heaven of higher math-
        ematics low athm, palms pressed on the floor. Gesture
was all there was I was learning, the noncombinatorial
                                                    hang
        of it given my wrist, a realm of what else could be...
    All eyes were on the floataway grist it got, a proposi-
tional feint, an oak handle wrapped in duct tape taken
                                                    out.
    One might've said or might as well have said, "Riddle
        me, riddle me," the troupe or the entourage we now
were by now bewildered. All eyes were up a tree, the aban-
    doned boy the bird we'd be, shot down as in Lamming's
                                                    book.
    In the dungeon of our skin we looked on listening, all
    eyes on the athmic all ears. To look was to hear the woods'
        whisper, Thad's wood's reckoning, the requisite con-
tour, crux. To look was to sniff with our comedic beaks. A
                                                    field
    as much as a feeling we had, we the rare birds caught the

smell of blood athwart the perfumed forest, the Dogon origi-
nary seed played upon it seemed, posthumous regalement of

                                                        Po

  its evolvement
seemed

Po flown was the seed on a sparrow's tongue. It wasn't
   Dogon Po except looked at a certain way, the way athm
staged it, transmigratory sheaves backed up or bodied
                                               forth.
   I popped up feeling I'd fallen from a tree. The bough
bent letting me down or a cop shot me, mystic and profane
   afflictions ran parallel tracks... In Thad's realm we were
                                               trees
   come back to life. In Hank's we were Ed Love's metal
monstrances, one of us hung from a poplar, one of us one of
   the Jes' Us's, of late no longer strange, of late in the open.
                                         Mobley
and Mosley stepped into a basement or a subway, stepping
   lightly downward à la LKJ, electric or acoustic stairs leading
                                           the
way

Dogon Anonymous

—"mu" two hundred seventy-third part—

Dogon Anonymous loomed high on its
  hill, a broad building with an eroding look.
To beat back the dry-throated dead was its

                                      prom-
  ise, no more dying of thirst. Stay-at-Homes
its occupants would be, none of them packed
  away in ships. A projection from the inside the

                                         hill
  it seemed... Such were its givens they'd make
    an old man shimmy, big-boy pants pulled up
up to below his nipples, a new Cab Calloway. One

                                       was
  to be done with Ogotemmêli, bid cloth and con-
cealment goodbye, about Sirius's companion star say
  nothing. One was to have no truck with the eight

                                       an-
  cestors, whatever truck was, ditto the Nummo
twins. What truck was remained a question, the
  supreme gnosis having truck, whatever it was, not
having truck... So went one's musings, caught up

                                       in
  sway, caught up in swirl, the building itself, it
seemed, indigenous to the hill. The question of
  truck remained a question, one we let slide or let

                                       sub-
  side, let go unanswered, day one of Dogon re-
covery dragging on. Was truck substance and
  silhouette's arcane wedding, the birds wanted

                                                    to
know, Andreannette's above-and-below-the-waist
     bounty inside a gauzy dress... There though I
   was, it seemed I lived less for then than for later,
                                                  the
     uppity birds out of 'Attar's book nested between
my ears, uppity but wise one was told. Andreannette's
     dress loomed as did the Dogon Anonymous build-
ing, a revival or a circus tent whose hem I crawled out
                                                      from
     under, saying the birds were killing me. Unlike the
dress, truck made of no truck, Dogon Anonymous
   offered solace, torment's extinguishment. No talk
                                              of
   the loom would there be, no talk of the smith,
 no talk of the loincloth. The sat-upon snake's head,
                                                we
   were assured, would not
come up

The birds were unremitting, merciless. "Beaks
    what had been kisses," they chirped, quoting me
to myself. The hardness of the beak said it all,
                                            the
    pointedness of it as well. They pit the snug-
        ness of the loincloth against Andreannette's
dress's loose fit, my head set spinning by the
    contrast, a kind of withdrawal setting in... The
                                            re-
    cursiveness of late life, I thought, time's in-
    exhaustible reach into itself, a fold as of cloth and
    yet another and yet another, the tightness of the
                                            loin-
cloth moot

            •

The birds had been chirping for ages, the
hoopoe and its hectoring crew. Day one of
   Dogon recovery would never end. The birds

                                    had

   become proponents of late-stage lyric...
"Andreannette's panty line leaves its mark
   on every hand," they said to the men of our

                               group,

   talk so heavy it took us by surprise. We were
   among the living, exchanging pleasantries,
glad to be alive. The wonder flesh could adorn

                               bone

   and both go forth we couldn't get over, late-
stage lyric ever on our tongues already, ever
   on our tongues anyway... Why were the Stay-

                               at-

   Homes no match for the Ravagers they were
still asking, the aural counterpart of silhouette
   maintained by a glottal hum below their talk of
Andreannette. They spread their wings and flew,

                               cir-

   cling high, showing off, thereness a matter of
   going-toward, tonal motion, aerial substance to
aural silhouette. We looked up wary of the sun,

                               eyes

   up using our hands for shade, only a fallen feath-
er whence color came left on the ground. Was the
   sun itself a bird we wondered and were looking to

                               see,

   the exact flame not to be looked at or seen but
suggested, the snugness of the loincloth an analogue,

                               Do-

   gon re-
lapse

There was to've been no talk of Griaule or Die-
    terlen. The birds would not oblige. Why did
the Stay-at-Homes mind their own business, they

                                            want-
    ed to know, not go asking far away from home.
Why didn't the men leave the women at home,
    why didn't they carve them on the bows of their

                                            ships,
    the birds chattered asking... Dogon Anonymous
        lay near the fallen feather now, the hill it was
on an anthill, genital as of old, word of which was

                                            not
    to be uttered but
was

Peter Gizzi

Now It's Dark

No one gave me a greater thing
than their time.
But the old song,
worn from use,
is with me again.
So much of it
behind me now.
In front of me a slow season,
when a face passes
into a name.
Last night the moon was lolling
9 degrees over the horizon
but I didn't know.
I was in a fever dream
downloading ravens into my skull.
An unkindness of them.
This is called what it's like
to sleep alone for years.
It means all these years to remain
untouched wrote the poem.
I use my mouth to say goodbye,
fever dream, raven, skull.
To say like a flower, little dust.
To say what of it.
The world is close today
and elegy is my tonic.

I recast language in hope
of recovering the red oak
my neighbors felled.
It lived over a hundred years, glowing.
Now, neither music or rhyme,
just night, tin, and sky.

Out of the World in Real Time

The silence in this room is causing a looping effect.

All I see is wood grain and air when it's raining in the true north
of the poem.

It gives purchase to the page. It gives courage.

I want to tell you this isn't just all song.

I want to say this scrap of paper has sky in it.

To be lost in its yesterglow casting shadows upon a silent h.

H for hour and honor, honest and heir, also ghost, ghastly,
ghetto, etc.

Who knew such light could come from torn paper.

What comes first, flag or paper? Voting or votive?

There are distances. The whole archival light blooming.

I recast words to say everything touched by light remembers
that light.

To recast light that touched marble strewn from time, lying
among weeds and trash—

worn from human traffic and ordinary songs.

In my head, a flywheel unable to power anything other than song and all that's left is survival—

some old piece of canvas flapping in the gale.

The oak creaks and the air is keening.

That green light could only be oxygen.

I am witness, a copy of rain in June, a glinting vowel.

Michael Earl Craig

Sprezzatura

To put your nose so far up another's ass
that your ears bend,
that your eyes water,
that your heels lift off the ground
a bit, as you press in there
so hard you do something
permanent to your cheek bones.
It is the nature of Nature.
It is a mysterious talking bow being lifted.
It is the bow string being drawn
(two callused fingers)
and tall grasses, flattened by the wind.
The drinking of iced tea from a hollow log.

Candlesnuffer

Dogs on chains drag their small huts across the tundra.
Men in fluffy flannel pants are kneeling.
Opposite calmnesses interact.

Driving Home

Hundreds of finches in road
resting, drinking from puddles.
As I drive through them &
they flutter up like sacred
soapflake eunuch moths
I think of the gaudiness of poetry.

End Times

Scrawny blind horses with stiff horse-dicks resembling ball bats
roam the plains from Vegas to Albany... big dicks banging on
old bathtubs and sagebrush. A few of you foresaw this.

A flattened glove on the barn floor, speckled with bird shit.
The transistor radio with dead batteries plays no Chopin.

An Arm Moving Quickly Through

a Coat Sleeve Lined with Taffeta

The caddy hefted his divot absentmindedly.
In two out of three of my nightmares I
am grilling a flank steak.
A single lewd limerick changed the mood of the evening.

Nick Twemlow

from *The 19th Technique*

> Note: This is an excerpt from *The 19th Technique*, a novel-in-progress. The story is straightforward: the narrator, an 11-year-old former child prodigy in martial arts, travels with his Mum to a karate tournament in Oklahoma City with the single purpose: to kill his father, who ran out on the two of them a few years prior, and had developed the narrator into the ultimate fighting machine by subjecting him to daily daylong training regiments that would destroy most adult martial arts masters.

Now's the time I should probably tell you that I was once considered a child prodigy. Most child prodigies flame out by the time they become adults, mostly because of the heavy burden they carry to fulfill the wishes of the cadre of adults who live their pestilent lives through child prodigies.

Most child prodigies are good at things that involve their brains. Some of them are discomfortingly good at playing musical instruments. Some have precocious vocabularies and can solve complex problems, often math related. Some are really advanced in a sport, like golf or tennis.

If the child prodigy is spotted early enough, they get to be on television talk shows. Adults love watching children do adult things. This is why adults employ children to work in factories.

I once asked my father, as he gazed at and diddled with his phone over dinner, if he thought about the little girls and boys who worked 12-hour shifts grinding down their fingertips to make the screen he was losing himself (and his family) to. He grunted, as if he had simultaneously heard me and concluded my question was irrelevant to his foregoing concerns.

I asked him again and he turned to me and told me that he once looked up that very question and learned that most of the little children who work in the factories that make his specific phone actually work eight-hour shifts and that many of them go on to management positions at the very factories where they begin working as early as age seven.

He admired these children, he continued. Look at you, he said to me. You're nine and what kind of management position are you setting yourself up for? This was one of the last conversations we ever had.

Some child prodigies appear to be obsessed with samurai movies. I don't really know why this is the case, but I have read two books in which this is so.

One of them is even called *The Last Samurai*. It's about a really smart boy who lives in London and watches samurai films with his Mum. His Mum, which is what you call a Mom when you live within the crown colonies, doesn't know who his father is, so the child prodigy seeks out several men who could possibly be his father, engages them in witty conversation, and then makes a decision whether or not he is his father.

The other book I read about a child prodigy obsessed with samurai films is called *Down the Rabbit Hole.* The narrator is a self-identified smarty-pants who reads the dictionary and is obsessed with hats and samurai films. By the end of the novel, he basically becomes a samurai, sort of. His dad is a drug lord and there are lots of corpses in the book. The thing is I was a child prodigy, too and you'd think, given that my genius was in the performance of various leg and hand moves designed to kill—meaning karate—that I, too, would be obsessed with samurai films. That isn't the case. If it matters, I'll speak more about that later.

Right now, I'm sitting in the car, still waiting for Mum to return from her stained glass group. She took up staining glass a few months ago. She also introduced me to Bob around this time.

Bob owns a toy store. He doesn't like it when I refer to it as a toy store.

He says that referring to what he sells as toys is akin to referring to a dentist or a chiropractor as a doctor. I don't understand the nuance. Privately, when Mum is in the other room with Bob, I refer to him as the owner of a toy store. Usually, I refer to him this way to Maxine, who usually just takes in what I have to say with virtually no expression.

I sometimes wonder if Maxine's head is full of lint. I once told Maxine that I wanted to stick a sidekick into and through my father, to feel his lungs and heart and blood squish through my toes, and she just sat there, expressionless. I think maybe Maxine doesn't register any obvious emotion because she lost her husband several years ago.

He's not dead, mind you; he left Maxine for one of his patients. This patient had been "cured" according to Maxine's husband; so technically, he wasn't violating any kind of law or ethic. His patient was, obviously, twenty years younger than Maxine, who was twenty years younger than her husband. Now, Maxine lives in our basement. She sits with me a lot, makes hot tea, and is a really good listener.

The kinds of games Bob sells are board games. He doesn't sell any kind of video game, which is why Bob is always borrowing money from Mum. He's a purist, he tells anyone who will listen. He was a child prodigy too, he once told me.

He was the best checkers player at his age in the whole world, when he was eight. I made the mistake of pointing out to him that being world class at checkers was like being good at watching television. I further noted that there has never been anything like a prodigy at checkers. If he had said he had been a world-class chess player as a child, I would've taken him more seriously. Bob pretty much won't really talk to me anymore.

I've never asked Mum why she chose to learn how to stain glass. Two of her recent works sit on our mantle, above our non-working fireplace. Both are square shaped, about two feet by two feet. One of them appears to depict a tree, though it could be the Eiffel Tower, which is the place Mum often thinks about, mostly because she's never been there and she once told me she's also never been in love.

I asked her about her marriage to my father, which lasted 12 years, and she always smiles in a rueful way, if that's possible, and says things like "It was a sham," or "Who could ever love that man?" When she said that last one, I noted that I once had, and she noted how I used the words "once had," and we entered into a complicit silence.

The other square of stained glass featured abstract color patterns: red, blue, and purple. It looked like a Kandinsky.

Kandinsky was painter who revolutionized the use of color in painting. He also was part of a group called Der Blaue Reiter, which is German for The Blue Rider.

I love this fact, largely because several people formed a group that refers to a singular person. If I ever form a group in protest of something— which is becoming increasingly likely, given my hatred of the way the martial arts is practiced and peddled these days—I will also confer upon it a singular referent. This will confuse people, especially our enemies.

Or maybe, since I have no respect for any living marital artist and therefor will likely form a group of one to protest, I will employ the opposite approach: I will name my group as a multitude. This will confuse my enemies just as much, maybe even more. They will think, when they hear I am coming, that I contain multitudes. I will call my protest group: The Abyss Is Coming.

Federico Italiano, translated by Brenda Porster

Hotel Libreville

The warm jungle heat
seeps into the lobby
dragging itself like a cloth
over the surface of things.

A waiter brings a brandy:
I looked for you at the bottom of this memory,
not mine, in the worn pages
of a transitory edition,

according to which we split up half-way through
the novel, or maybe even before,
when we walked back along the cliff
that night, without a flashlight,

because there were no more ferry boats
and no other tongue would ever translate us.

Alexis Orgera

Multiple Choice Test

Facsimile thereof. Hyperextension.
Hero worship. Bilateral longing.
Hope for another future.
Spinal aperture. Nerve ablation.
Fixed-gear thinking. Systems analysis.
General fascination. Bird in hand.
Burning bush. Hapless road trip.
Design engineering. Folic acid.
Rendered self. Remodeled kitchen.
E-dream. Record-breaking flight.
Ocean liner. Rental home.
Compendium stream. Google search.
Vague description. Workshop sawhorse.
Heavenly sphere. Slips of paper.
Dictionary definition. Detonation
switch. Incendiary verb.
Speech pathology. Egress, ingress.
Blood vessel pathway. Heart attack.
Desire-storm. False idol.
Tweaked blueprint. Secret passage.
Glowing door in a dark hall.
Foundational knowledge.
Hope monger. Night whisperer.
Comma lover. Three crows
chasing a hawk. Stonecutter.
Cheese grater. Dinnertime.

Krystal Languell

If You Succeed, We Will Destroy You

title by and poem after Howardena Pindell

What we said about the grid
was various and not simple

The paper dots sometimes fell loose
Unstretched material waves up

The stitches beneath the layers
got wider and gappier over time

Mixed-media feels wide and warm
No disguising ideas after the injury

Or how the work would be shipped
more like a sculpture than a painting

We wondered at the materials' origins
Her tool selection, dot and glitter size

Later she used their language in collage,
the warnings to comply abut her figure

When the boss says have a nice day
Understand it means eat shit and die

Howardena's turning to the cosmos
outside the market diagramming stars

Emily Hunerwadel

peach woman

She's saying   what's been true recently
        this vehicle   and street lights like angler fish
a body that buckles the scene around it
        the meteor-less   truth of me

She's saying   the punishment is forgetting
that poems are funerals for the present
        and we are a people
who mark our territory with tears

and meanwhile,   rain in a sulphur town
        red clay made redder by brake light
the world does its revolution
                and the odometer promises
        all leaving is returning

She's saying   becoming horizonless
        is a matter of cruelty to the sky
that illusion upstages the record
        that in our infidelity to the night
we dreamed awake the things
                we couldn't see in our sleep

peach woman

she's saying I'm over this memetic carrying on
       and my swimming eyes   like red ink

this winter is a series of baths   and I've now
become accustomed   to who she is in pictures:
      smoke in Shasta,   more glitter than mirror

and I'm saying this scenic route   snaking its way
to our bar-stool storyline,   where she's
the condensation she's speaking into   puddles on the table

and meanwhile the friends in their orbits and
the questions we throw at the sky,   my routines without her,
      half real with faces on the screen
the return of some draft   I made of this desire

peach woman

I'm wanting to say primordial ooze but it's all
coming out broken compass needle, protagonist
friend I mean starlight but it's instead the story
in which you throw up in the bushes If I'm
wanting to dream peonies hatched like eggs
apocalypse as apex My mouth is trying heaven
but says height I'm meaning to start something
like a crumbling I'm trying to smile on one foot
I'm aiming to love you like a rabbit in the road
I'm wanting to tell you yes with my hands

Ryan Mills

Thunder of A Thousand

I took a selfie in the mortuary bathroom. Visitors enjoying their mini caprese & deviled eggs, slightly warm. Slightly ham sandwiches. Uncomfortable in their dresses & neckties. I made a slightly seductive face, unshaven yet showered. I thought to say killing it, thought better of it. I thought to wash my hands in the washbasin. Thought I'd taste the shrimp. In conversation with distant relatives, is there blood? Who will help to shake this paprika? The shrimp will not be saved. The dead in their favorite overalls and sporting team shirts. No longer in their uniforms. What is the uniform for tomorrow? The disease and the daisies. Milking daisies out of the plastered clouds. East gun White neck East gun White neck.

Corinne Dekkers

As Snakes Do

there is the loss of something and then there is the loss of
something else something could be said to be time or
something could be said to be a person or something
could be said to be a person in a time or something could
be said to operate as undercurrents   sorted
broadcasting hand seed and kelp and that grapple could
be Fiji could be rosed if there could be another work for it
could discern itself and could be nothing under every corner
and under every edit   so that when you do believe yourself
to be further from this   you will descend
as snakes do   liquid in your movement
          smoke or gas falling
                  like waters do   to ask
                          what did I do with
                  the water   where did I
          move it   too is there a medicine
          here for this
                  passing   and if so where will I swallow
                          winging mallow   blue
                          for you   your rye
                          and your room
                                  a stretch on the Hudson

Mark Anthony Cayanan

The Wilderness Was the Time Between Prophets

Not we but the material world, ungenerous surface
we harrow over and over. Not we but
our mud-caked fingers scratching holes into our skulls, in this heat
we are everything we feel. Not we but gunshots let loose
in the night before night untangles itself
from its told stories. Not we but before this unfamiliar century, one
traffic light debilitating the plaza, we would give
way as we're selfless, we're too much
time. Not we but yearly and half a millennium in
we rid the saint's raiment of dust, wipe our fingerprints off
the glass casket. Not we but patience
though patience has no value in this life, and we worry
though won't ever say it to each other
there isn't another life we deserve. Not we
but a landscape that fits the loneliness of waiting long
and for what. Not we but without the savior's promise
there's only a crowd without reason. Not we but
in the same space, exchangeable bodies, the mountain we've made
is a mountain made of paste. The infinite
has the transparency of evil, the lynched
herald said. Not we because not infinite, not evil
in a manner that's important. Not we but a competition
for piety, a priest in every family, every unmarried daughter

a nun. To be young is to virgin. Not we but the high-noon

       shadow of a minor basilica. Not we but penance in behalf of

         methodists and communists, though we're all

children, some are born better than others. Not we

      but magician and scientist, theologian and hypnotist, mob

        psychologist and hunger artist, the prophet

who shall come shall make the sun dance and mouth

     bleed, not we but the skittish sun.

The New Abandon

1

When the priest sees the new prophet sinking into prayer, floating in mid-air, he tugs them down by the shirt.

2

When the priest who doesn't possess the angel's tongue sees the new prophet sinking into prayer for the seasonal workers, floating in mid-air, mind wandering up the unpaved roads where dwell the farmhands, he tugs him down by their shirt.

3

The plaza brims with holiness when the priest who doesn't possess the angel's tongue opens the cathedral doors. He sees the town lurch toward the new prophet sinking into prayer, their flesh invaded by pains borrowed from the seasonal workers, spirit floating in mid-air, mind wandering into basketball courts where teenagers exhaust their hungers, up the unpaved roads where dwell the farmhands. Though their spirit is true, they tug themselves down by their body, the ill-fit shirt, the sturdy error.

4

The plaza brims with impatient holiness when the priest who doesn't possess the angel's tongue opens the cathedral doors and lets out the scent of roses. He sees the town lurch toward the new prophet and feels the wraith-breath of their corruption, feels it pronounce his years. May the prophet sinking into prayer be the one corruption the faithful love together. May their flesh be invaded by pains borrowed from the seasonal workers, pains the great design that outlasts us, their spirit floating in mid-air surpass the private life nurtured without our knowledge. Though their mind fails to outstrip their age, their name continues wandering into basketball courts where teenagers exhaust their hungers, up the unpaved roads where dwell the farmhands. Though their spirit is true they release them. And when they tug themselves back down by his body, the ill-fit shirt that's costume, whose will preserves the sturdy error that gave them their flesh, drives them to love torment?

5

Because redemption precedes ruin, the plaza brims with impatient holiness and gossip when the priest who doesn't possess the angel's tongue opens the cathedral doors and lets out the scent of roses. Those hawking bottle-green passerines and scapulars stop for the minor wonder. He sees the town lurch toward the new prophet, toward another new abandon, and feels the humid wraith-breath of their corruption on his skin, feels it pronounce his years with the intimacy of sin. May the prophet sinking into prayer be at least the one corruption the faithful love together, each person a history of insignificant failures, and then renounce. May their flesh be invaded by pains borrowed from the seasonal workers, let pains be from the great design that outlasts us, let the great design be the delicate version of the universe we architect in childhood. May their spirit floating in mid-air surpass the private life nurtured without our knowledge, within each day exists the necessary day, denying trespass. Though their mind fails to outstrip their age, their name continues wandering into basketball courts where teenagers exhaust their hungers, up the unpaved roads where dwell the farmhands, as far as the capital whose angers aren't the same as ours. Though prayer is prayer and belief, belief, there's saltwater in our hearts, we cast our nets and sweat, nightly we drag outriggers to the shore, no apparition exacting as need. Though their spirit is true they release them into the virgin's words, the promise of her face, and when they tug themselves back down by their body, thirteen and always waiting, the ill-fit shirt that's their uniform of devotion and costume of commerce, whose will preserves the gunpowder threat of our future, frayed gauze of all afterlives? The sturdy error that gave them their flesh drives them to their knees, here where everyone's desperate to be loved back with a god's love, to master this masterable torment.

Rachelle Rahmé

Wifi DNA

Give a rat a cigarette butt

Yellow lines on the cement and bits of old blackened gum

Buildings still for sale

Chicks hanging out having a drink

I forgot it's Friday

In which the officers plan to be out and armed

No beer in that deli, I walk in and out, they're probably used to that

People and life go on

They say we're creating more trash, that's impossible, impossible, fake, what

There's no more movies, no more ushers sweeping up popcorn, collecting abandoned drinks and candy, sometimes a mini-bar bottle, no more, theme parks, slushies and greasy powdered plates of stale funnel cake, it's none of that garbage

Impossible, fake, so it seems

Brushes pushing away yesterday's ashes

Detailing the Audi RS6, washing it caressingly with soft bristled paint brushes and non-abrasive suds

The triangle of concrete bombarded with yellow rays, one brimming with grasses

Veronica Martin

The Baby Teeth Smile Up the Street at Ragged-Toothed History

The most beautiful thing I saw in the month of January
was this tooth that appeared in my palm, having fallen from the fold
of my travel wallet at an early hour of the morning. I was in Rome.
The sun had not yet risen. I'd been looking for the number for a taxi
who had not kept its appointment, so I was standing fixed and frantic
before the phone in my marble-toned apartment just off the Piazza de Spagna,
on the Keats-Shelley side. I was going home, though the taxi had other ideas.
I ran out into the Roman night to flag down a car, my luggage lodged
at the bottom of the thin baroque stairway discreetly keeping the door open,
so I did not have time to think about the tooth, and I told myself as much,
staring at it for that moment by the phone, sharp and small and human, laying
in the deepest part of my palm. This being when another part of intelligence
kicks in. Rome becomes the room you, as a child, were instructed to carry
the glass of water across without spilling. Knowing utopia exists for an hour,
    at best a day.

The Recitation

The most beautiful thing I saw in the month of April
was this mosquito perched lightly upon thin skin
stretched across the cheekbone of a poet I'd just met at a party.
She was in her 70s. Speaking about her life. Instead of brushing
the insect away I watched as her animated face lifted it and let it down
and how it, resolutely, remained fixed in place. Perhaps it was feeding.
But I didn't think so. All around us other poets were engaged in other
conversations. Everyone was drinking. Together, we moved more deeply
into the night. The poet and I went to a pair of chairs in the corner, below
windows that rose at a slant over our bowed heads. She began to cry.
I had lost track of the mosquito. Before the party broke, a few poets took it on
to remember a few lines from other poets. When there was nothing left
to say or to remember everyone got into their passenger seats or slipped behind
    their wheels,
wound back down the mountain toward the perfect thing of the valley.

Megan Savage

Regeneration

The face of Dog Mountain, that turn from dead plane,
slices of translucent sun about my feet.

Rustle in the depth hoar. The pull in the pack
and the snap of wind in my face.

One summer in Montana I tried to capture
the last of the glacier ice, so small

your head in my lens obscured it. The germ of a lesion had
formed inside me, but we did not know it.

All sublimation begets unclassifiable forms:
cups, scrolls, columns, ribs that bind our hearts

And the ringing. Above the treeline, rock. The hoarfrost
shows its grain. More crystal lattice than fragments of stars.

Regeneration appears first angular, then faceted. Light
bleeds through our skin, makes us three-dimensional.

Gabriel Palacios

Pavilion of Having Had Moments in a Tempe Mall Aquarium

Everyday I open up a newspaper
& there isn't an article
About what I think is the most important story in humanity:

Halfway now across my valleys
Of black tarp befalling kiosk, mirrorhouse of
Indistinguishable sandstone buttes, methanogenic manta

Surfing its own post-traumatic wind shear invisibly flat,
Convergently evolved
Under the arced shade of a planetary ring,

Under the whistle of its people's Ennio Morricone,

In this lighting I can see we build a generation starship just
To build it
In miniature.

What has changed what has ever changed what can be changed.
Nothing, nothing
Has been changed.

That horizon & the telescopic
Wife & child

Waving you inside

The murals of an ownership group past

Catherine Bresner

VAGABOND Agnès Varda, 1985, 106mins

in one scene the soft brown sand and the light on the sand and between
beach grasses a woman walking out of thin paper waves

in another the camera slow and careful, right to left, over each stone
made to make a wall and there she is with her chestnut hair all wild beside it

beside it a highway and we will sleep with men if we have toif the wandering
is too long or the gut aches, if the danger is thick and the drugs run out

the drugs will run out, black rubber tires, zeros, it is winter now and
now what will you do, you didn't choose the weather, but you chose the road

in one scene a hundred goats huddle in a barn waiting to be milked
she is alive and she is alone and the road is hers and she is not for milking

in another six cypress trees press their thumbprints against the sky
and Mona drifts among them
right to left to farther left to somewhere farther still

greasy canned beans, hunks of bread for sopping, in another scene
she is getting sick at the station
red wine sloshing, a telephone booth emergency

we will fall in love sometimes despite ourselves, a red scarf, we think this love
will save us and we joan of arc ourselves into catastrophes

some human kindness must be required, some human kindness and
a soft beach, crisp waves, some chipper sandpipers, perhaps a warm sun
a peopleless beach, a warm sun, a sand dune, some brown kelp, a few rocks
some human kindness in that famous dark

ashtray in the mouth, a woman prays only to exist, peacefully the dirt waits
to be dug, and she is alone and the road is endless and she is drunk by it

Brandi Katherine Herrera

from *MOTHER IS A BODY*

Here's a tip: use a mirror, or a microscope. Notice your own mammalian self. Just don't look too closely — that way, if the egg turns into a fox or a rabbit, you won't know the difference. Note the dark center of the female body: the one that evolved out of the boy character and his mother character. You know what I mean? Everyone's involved here. The whole head of the seed of the father of all young women swells until the pronuclei merge. And then it's complete! Our bodies dance and dance and then they cut each other down. In general, that's what the act of mating is.

Zach Savich

easthampton

D. says forty-five leaves is the rule of thumb for each apple so perfectly I
    am recalling marksmen winnowing additional leaves from a bough in a
    film of archery as a child
a fox thrums the gravel brink
I watched until I heard *thrums the gravel brink*

is there hot water left or hot water again
or swerving to avoid apples in the road in the mirror seeing children in the
    road move the apples in the mirror so the next driver cannot avoid
let the middle be composed by another

it's only indispensable sprinkler on in rain boats on a busted reservoir
    formal dances in improvised films
the winner is
congratulations

I Built

I built the house around the chimney built around a tree   I left the
ladder in saplings   a decade later I saw it   between the music   aloft
(lightning broke the angel's trumpet off at the wrist)   (the mouth appears
singing)   like that you said like what just all of it

--

how did you sleep   (did you sleep)   the circuit burns out as soon as it
fires   it can fire for a while though   the suits we made to endure the
unendurable fire could not   so we made them prettier   and for longer
(lives have been changed by less)

Joyelle McSweeney

Deathstyles 12.8.20

the blondes

Even on this cold plump date I see above me
a vision of a maiden bleeding from the septum-- I mean a teen dream
with ironed hair streaking flatly away -- up the sightline
of a schoolgirl with her sharp chin pointing up
a cold sheer nasal corridor canting steeply away from us
wherein you could squint to make out an uppermost crack
where in wind could blow like light
and manifest trashily
trash that can leave and be swept up on wind
we so devoutly wanted
to leave and be swept up in
get trashy
and ultimate
on the high vinyl mat left out behind the highjump
where the track edged on some kind of shaggy nursery
baking there abandonedly
swoop of sun-in can't lift the hair too dark for it
picking plastic shredded coating off the paperback
temporary perfection
via an array of inhalable minipoisons
like a bat this vision materializes out of the morning
to swoop in the long hallway of the school
an inky penstroke, stroke sequellae on a scan
a brighter version of the wind
to sling a book at and bring down
first I was hit by the door then the doorjamb

then I came in swinging
in the basement the band rotated like junk saints
in the garage some guy blinked then touched two wires together
cured in the formaldehyde of our collapsible classroom
we ran out on the mesa to watch the storm arrive
I lay down on the picnic table and let my braids drain
and the live oaks rise
I lay down lithe in the edison bulb
and took the current
ethelrosenberg
ethylalchohol
ethelcalledsusie
my first cousin's name
and once removed
it was a youthful fantasie, starring me, a neverblonde
the whole smashed-up edition of the faerie queen
reverted to pulp soaked in vodka in the gut
onlie to arise again on the gullet
of a depressive aromatic lady voter
also me
with a sash around my waist with a loaf
of stolen stollen on my arm
for gods above a gloating Wotan
the glabrous gold sigil of the Wu-Tang clan
dozing on its flagstaff
practiced attitudes of dismay my resting expression
and yes it rose that way
and froze
my face
the clapper of the poppet in the clock
resting by the quarter hour
smiling for nobody in the dark
when the weathergirl arrives
(her miniskirt, her ironed hair)

each task or committment
explodes its combustible husk
in the flare-y sudden cargo of the truck--
          it took me getting hi-lo
it took me turning that dial this way and that
it took me crashing that truck
it took me getting this dent in my brow
it took me getting my head caved in
it took me cashing in my accounts
it took me getting clocked like this
it took me wearing the deep cleft around
like the hoofprint of the aleph-ox
or the bird's back when its wings are spread
or any other suggestive and aromatic cleft
it took me turning my ear to it
to struggle for signal
unhasping my jaw and discarding it
it took me fumbling with the fillet knife
my knuckles frozen in the rime
on the shipboard cannery
between gigs as a student and a sea instructor
with my bouie knife and my ghillie knife
it took me being this one grainy stripe of white
in the muscle
just one briefy knotted tendentious stripe
easier to cut
away
than this cold semi-solid oracular feeling
that is both liquid and more-than-ice
some kind of incredible mind-stage sluicing through
from the ambiguity of god-language
to flood the mucky guts that flood the deck
with the certainty
of doing something wrong of doing something wrong

eightminutes for the water to boil
alphabet noodles for the kids soup
or whatever returns to earth
whatever needs to come back here
to earth
has eight minutes
Mr Sunshine
whatever we hurled up into the troposphere
has to return
any weather arriving
any messenger from the gods
when we thought we were through with it--
any invisible chemical soupiness that
smelled like cleanliness and
spelled out drastic riddles
in the drain
melting baby sock in the dryer
becoming particulate
entering air
and entering art
and telling no secrets
and going nowhere
then raining back down again like a clockwork
for the baby to inhale
like everything that ran down around my ankles to tell me
in the rightness of that concentrated cold
the coldness of garbage swiling in the gutters
money seemed to need an icehouse, a bank to live in
but really it was everywhere and nowhere at once
like that god who couldn't commit
but rained gold sometimes when he felt like it
who you were always fucking in the shower

Jan Verberkmoes

Charadrius mongolus schaeferi / Lesser Sand Plover /
Mongolenregenpfeifer

[33° 50′ N, 97° 10′ E]

between the lung and sixth
lung

after stones among eggs
in sand

hot how
      ell
      shells   of light crackling

      blue wind skims
      blue wi
            underheard

between the black crane fall
und wasser

der sand knis   istert zwischen
water and air

  cranes of failing-light
  lunging

between one egg collapsing and none

where one lung
closes the next

between blackfall and
the neck rolling

there you are *zwischen*
and we e

steep skim
shi   until shining

and there you were *knis*
        and   now

From 1934-36, German zoologist and SS officer Ernst Schäfer and American naturalist Brooke Dolan II conducted a natural history expedition across Tibet and China—their second of the decade. They collected roughly 3,000 birds over the course of this trip, including species and subspecies new to Linnaean taxonomy. The birds were then transported back to the Academy of Natural Sciences in Philadelphia and the Museum für Naturkunde Berlin, where they remain today.

Jeffrey Yang

from *Langkasuka*

10

Words spoken, words written
Words so easy to understand and so easy to put into practice
Yet no one can understand them and no one can put them into practice
Words have their ancestor and affairs have their sovereign
People unused to the way are unwilling to understand them
When a few understand we will surely be honored
And so the poets, in worn rags, conceal a priceless piece of jade within

48

In the beginning, God gave Gabriel
the Breath of Life to pass to Adam.
Adam's body was still lifeless earth
and water, when the archangel flew
down to place the Breath by his nostrils
and animate him. But Gabriel, wanting
to see the Breath, opened his hands
and the Breath escaped, becoming
hantu, disembodied spirits, the older
siblings of humankind who dwell in darkness,
while the children of Adam live in the light.
Invisible air and fire, sometimes envious,
and if accidentally disturbed, vindictive,
hantu are propitiated through the *main
peteri* rite. Some say the Breath went up
Adam's nostrils and he sneezed, scattering
the Breath across his body. His body was
too weak for the Breath, which broke
into little fragments. God told Gabriel
to weld (*peteri*) the fragments back together,
and so the *main 'teri* healing rituals weld
people together through play (*main*),
making sick people well. And the Wind,
the anthropologist said, blew inside her
own chest with the force of a hurricane.

Joshua Pollock

Untitled

I dug up a hole and it sang for me

the air awakened

enguided to the body, unusuable hands

and it goes—abandoning with wild abandon

a black tahr ascends an escarpment of vein-laden limbs

I erected an edifice on a discursive subduction zone

the mantle liquifies while the boring machine seizes, crazily

exchange of cusp looks, crepuscular, at the edge of phase shift, loss or
    cast loose

the interstitium spent history hidden right below the skin

a spigot spits rust-water into track ballast

crunch of boots, early fog, a figure from behind, burdened internally

overnight the sky collapsed overnight something died

overnight the village burned or the milieu was unraveled and executed

there is the call of a horse

snarling dogs

a mirror dimension shares the size and shape of our space

I abhor my addiction to abyss and to void

the casting of accidental sex hexes, words emerge

in a contusive voice,

and improbably, a hummingbird drags me out of my head

speed drips,   at the train station,   a body trapped in another time

I don't know which will sting worse

a slow cool to tepid stasis or rapid, ardent immolation

ferocious thoughts, never unhappening, something blurted tentatively

something like a cloud

to see life with impossible perspective, front and side at once,

as if painted on a curved plane

the last thing I want is to be captured by context

Kristi Maxwell

DIBATAG

an extinction

welcome, wholesome voyeurs—
Lowell's-skunk wholesome, empresses of crème,
who prefer sour over funky or choose lower volumes
for love's solos (love commonly over-performs)

here, envy mooches off chlorophyll's work,
sponsors chlorophyll's one-sun show (essence: chlorophyll hoovers
specks of sun plus resourcefully reuses—surely, our clumsy folklore

ensorcells)—see cooks fume over flourless roux ("no such slurry!")
(self's own slur)

when ozone chokes up, we console—
over here's our mock-up of numen
for our new elsewhere
where scenes of men show no cloven hooves

keep up: even foyers where we queue look lonesome
loosen now your peels, unlock your sunken forms

' AKEKE ' E

an extinction

conscious of nightly symbols forming on historic forts

        how to unfold   unmoor   unmission

to join   issuing forth your country into my country

so hot so unbound   not occupying but simply   touching

      my own tropic cools   this fusing isthmus shorts

                           dibs on unwounding

        stop this posturing   this conviction disposition

           dust-gluttonous   tumor-thorough

thoroughly mining this bituminous night for lost hours

pumicing our moon's bright foot

          involving full-grown minors or mirrors in this whodunit

trying not to but noticing   this world's voluminous booty

        flossing with history's thong

    with history's wrongs   showing

      monolithic thoughts build phobic logics

        it's on us to unbuild

          clog this porous wisdom

          with your good or mostly good oil

Justin Phillip Reed

BUT THE CROSS IS ONLY AN IMPLEMENT OF TORTURE. ITS SHADOW IS THE DARKNESS IT CASTS, YOU SEE. NOTHING CAN SURVIVE THE SHADOWS.

Shadows come in crews. Consider Solé in '99 in three light designs, six fans spinning 36 blades. A cut to her cuts her slim figure-8 into several Xs. WHODAT. Seven *I*s, twice, as in a sonnet of first-person assertion, the self ever forthcoming & possible; or a ballad stanza couplet of "aye" as in agreement, (the official affirmation of crews of real crooks in congress, but here) a fourteener of *fuckwimme* that is also *fuck outta here with that.* WHODAT? JT Money making money & love synonymous from fake & sophisticated restraints:

this is how I found copsplus.com & could BUY NOW Smith & Wesson double-locking, nickel-plated handcuffs for 20 dollars. If he hollers, let him breathe less loudly. Knuckles & nuts shadow me. Their badges signify a butterfinger & lazy eyes. I graduated from bullies to bullies with taxpayer backing & pensions. I put this psychological crisis of cringing at endless pursuit into a concrete poem the people thought was dark but fun. The darkness / The it / The castes in crosshairs I'm persuaded to reiterate for people who don't mix concrete & poetry can best be allegorized by what lurked on all surfaces that children with markers could find in the 90s: Möbius strips drawn out of six vertical bars & their shadows. My lyric involutes with my brain matter. In the myth, the labyrinth was essentially a prison. Imagine the U.S. allowing my mind to imagine leaving. All I do is think about you. I stick like a down ass chick.

From "Who Dat" to "Who We Be," what interests me is the consistent thrash of limbs against context. X's restless body, refusing to comply with the stasis of a cell, breaks monotony into montage. His litany upsets the limits of the frame. But is he

repeating (percussing) "dead end" or what? while seven children,
blue & grayscale as the "us" Michael choruses "they don't really
care about," each declare "I am DMX." I I I I I I I sing myself into

the melismas K-Ci makes of the words "land" & "country" in a
video where him & Jo-Jo, in shiny leather & fish-eye shades, shuffle
from bunk to block—everything the light touches flooding them in
a motif of police presence. How the brothers end up crooning on
the roof in suits has me asking if Black people's panoptic self-
consciousness, born of coming into being under perpetual
surveillance, manifests in these visual emphases on omnipresence.

I was raised to believe that God & my dead daddy were always
watching. How does a Black expat? On this Möbius strip, empire &
I try to figure which of us is captive to the other, & neither grows
up.

Down at the cross stood more crosses. Out of a jackal came
Damien. "The snake, the rat, the cat, the dog. How you gone see em
if you living in a fog?" Shadows emerge in mobs. I mean, far from
barbecuing the swine in my mind, I'm still draggin the red wagon
in which rattle my uncles' knuckles, their gold cuspids, their brass
tacks, nuts & bolts, their cars on cinderblock, the ropes they show,
the concrete they pour, how their women pay. The days spread out
with the chocolates in our little pockets til there was no shortage of
grown ass men holding fistfuls of formless dreams & aluminum
foil. In the shape of my life a stray dog tugs a radio flyer piled high
with a bastard

who removes a leather belt in perpetuity. The belt
is irreducible. It is also the leash. The animal
really gives a damn. The man's just good with his hands.

The crew in me accrues the crew in him, as well as
the deputy who tailed them & the confederacy
of foreman who boyed them the daylong before,

their fathers before them. All at least six feet.
In the six-month Carolina summer, their shadows
atop gravel lots at cookouts resemble drainage

where the got-loose dog was curb-popped & left to bloat.
They risk permanent damage when observed with the naked eye.

Arda Collins

September October

How many centuries equal gold pennies?

How many?

How many?

How many?

Suns or days

of fallen-down light?

Tossed, the stream

in the small woods

follows a plane of pebbles underwater

hundreds of years into the sun.

A soft day

on the banks where trees had fallen. Humid sunlight

after a storm. A new time set in.

Evening cools and smoothes.

Who is a penny in the river?

Who is a shiny rock?

Who is the water and who is the light?

A shiver, a love, one you miss, and a wish.

Where the riverbed is shallow

look in; pain shines, scatters, fades, and goes far away,

now driving a car on a parkway into sundown.

Shaded Road

My life seems short and uninteresting

but I like it.

Oh, this is something only I see,

my mind's short hop

back to where I had been,

a young, smiling, rounded face,

lonely and afraid.

Really though,

where am I?

A spool of thread,

the garden in the alley, evening,

dim as it courses

through my ears,

blood from stars.

Wish, Swish

A butterfly appears

out of the corner of your eye.

Somewhere, there is a painting.

A full sky, a face

pointed up, an angel

with a golden aura

pops out from one corner.

You do,

it comes in,

the mammoth particulate reality,

blood stationed everywhere

under a lignite sundown. A freight

of light, peat, ash;

an ocean, blue, like you.

A door chimes,

parietal, galactic,

inside a skull or two.

Alice Notley

Some Runes

1) You slipped through and left me but I
know everyone   I see your face
All you want is enough to make
the sun rise on you but if it
doesn't   and you slip back through, these
runes might be of use   you don't
really need them but the new dead
can be anxious like your babies
cried   Remember anything's more
than one and shifts   In your shift fol-
low me the rune through the keyhole
colored crow's wing or martin floats
without trying to any more

2) After a time your new body's
the old one that used to enclose
what you thought you were but you were
the greater body of thought   Thou
art thou   Yes you think I am me
Floating til you find after
the keyhole the heart of rubies
or soul the infinite clustered
presence of all and this rune you
hold now connects you to speaking
without vocal cords without ears
say it all at once in your mind
all these lines at the same moment

3) And all who've returned before you
say: we endlessly repeat with-
out trying this welcome while we

also do other floating things
Pull the word inside out and laugh
color with magenta your
next veiled partition   then it's clear
whatever you remember has
no past   it was made out of glass
nothing breaks here so take this rune
touch it when you might recall *mal*
it will cast your memory a-
mong every memory ever
had   will you find it again   (I'll
keep it for you in the clear heap)

4) Promised no future stay here for-
ever say any word you know
them all inscribed here on this rune
all of them upon it floating
down floating up evil love career
barrier live to grow dead weeds
what you may recall has no time
there be no tempest trick or trap
leaving the tradition go to
maps multidimensional con-
stellatory real to enter pearl
I went in there once and said that
I remember doing that
and sticking together into nameless

5) Where do I keep my runes wherev-
er you are with this one now too
doesn't this time ever stop no
this rune helps you shrug off old time
this is older time timeless time
to speak The Old Language calling
to it it calls back   it knows you
more than you know it but sing it
every note a hole we're composed
by no one at all it's scary
almost   but it's like every-

thing you always knew would be here
what the saints knew but also you
this rune or hole (holy) tells you

6) This rune is bottomless tele-
pathy spoken to me and you
says the colors are showing it
here's some red undangerous glass
words go dust, reoccur other
"I'm just in your mind so you can
think quick in response unpressured
don't you know that who you were is
this one you are?"   "is that enough?"
"there's no quantity" someone says
you still have a memory of
senses though you have pushed through them
they were tiny holes   find unedged
panes now this rune's for new sight too

7) This rune is medicine for grief
that once was five letters holding --
what you had to hold now I do --
I the maker   and holder of
what you once thought personal, now
vanished into my heart   do you
want it back   "no I still exist
so I don't need it." The flower
grows in gathered dark unreasoned
in floating darkness my terrain
in open stalls that are notes in
which I emerge and exist don't
you know you were always like this

8) I'm rune before The Old Language
Contradictory? I'm note/hole
I'm controls   Hold me and don't try
you go into twilight, emerge
blooming with leaves or other green
you will retain verdant beauty

go in HOLE sleep velvet come out
        NOTE
sudden sprouting green staff am I
holding it faces me singing
this holds you these notes   I'm rune/
HOLE you went in the hospital
you left with new musical key-
holes through which leaves slip and chant
the controls without knowing it

9) Something only means what's going
on here   inside's pure   if you still
feel guilty hold this rune   or if
you miss someone or thing use it
to find them and if they're alive
talk to them while they're asleep. I
first met you before you were born.
What are you like? You are marked and
you sing that inside you're inside-
out here   Alice found me and gives
me to you so you can be your-
self not definable a part-
icular enormity   dark
or light called by name or not

10) With this rune remake planet and
universe   I've been remaking
its substance transforming its part-
icles -- do they exist -- for eons
Is this rune only for the live?
Put it next to heart creating
keyhole to admit evil and
perform its purification
let it back out through keyhole
rendering us all more complex?
Understand I love you and use
complexity as new surface
I'm always converting your guilt
to texture and flow (I Alice)

124

11) I this rune was found by Alice
May twenty twenty   it ensures
The Old Language's passage un-
derneath your passages through
a time of disease   but you made
disease, this rune teaches, though who
could want it, my darling? it is part
of everyone's consuming each
other   In heaven you don't eat
or breathe you float   Now find your fears
Make a NOTE/HOLE amid them and
inside it rest floating like a sound
the sound of TOL   I make my-
self over and over from thought
its charming singsong expanse

12) Ghede guide me my friend to write
     this rune TO ANY, ME IN HAND:

I give it to you what you need
dead or alive, for it exists
even alive, even alive
touch this rune because it has it
the only thing you need just touch
if floating with your floating self
pwòp tèt ou Ghede says   I say
in TOL   which now appeareth
AS I AT FIRST COME TO BE NOW
as it is always happening
be with this one rune to be now
all you need is to be, you are

13) To know why you stick together
and move use me, rune . . . Where am I?
Where are you? I stick you together,
that's where you are. Do you remem-
ber who you are? I do it for

you, that's who you are. If someone
asks who you are say, I'm this rune.
Isn't that enough? Ghede says
you are my bèl memwa you are
my gravite . . . that is this rune is
I've stuck you together for all
your life and death   even when you
don't touch me   controls notes holes
what I am of, one, in krystal.

14) If you say that's so in crys-
tal each time saying makes it that
but you have to be right here where
there's nothing   I'm the rune that takes
you here   you've always been here but
things made of built matter get you
you think they're the here but they're not
the runes -- the controls -- stick you to-
gether   means it doesn't come from
analysis of built matter
be right here where there's nothing   to
have me   now go through a hole in
built matter   or just stay here crystal

15) This rune's medicine for extreme
sin   Ghede knows me he forgave
his brother   If I forgive you
it rips your sin out of you you
must start with nothing naked soul
if you don't choose forgiveness you'll
keep remembering what you did
I don't care what it is I don't
care about the bloody events
in the earth world of pain   You have
me if you want to forget tout bagay
everything   or you can keep
trying to recall something true

16) I am rune for real earth world I
show you reality's been e-
rased on earth until you see it
Use me to see no description
what you see's in The Old Language
and can be recalled   the dark wood
cubicles on a ceiling   walk
through these rooms from earth past later
that are shining smooth   because I
tell you that's what the real is   Cu-
bicles like runes to see in night
after death dark like light   Just look
everything has soul it's alive

17) There's no reason that you have al-
ways existed   you can't ask
what being is since there's no death
what that you did mattered it was
all matter nothing special un-
til you were exact in crystal
like now that you're dead   Hold me
after or in the world-of-pain
I'm as transparent as you are
gleaming for inside eyes   You've al-
ways known I'm the rune of this place
in you you've always known though not
remembered where you are yourself

FONO
GRAF

Fonograf Editions is a registered 501(c)(3) non-profit organization. Find more information about the press at: fonografeditions.com.